BERRY-DEE, Christopher

Killers on the web

KILLERS ON THE WEB

KILLERS ON THE WEB

TRUE STORIES OF INTERNET CANNIBALS, MURDERERS AND SEX CRIMINALS

CHRISTOPHER BERRY-DEE
AND STEVEN MORRIS

JOHN BLAKE

Published by John Blake Publishing Ltd,
3, Bramber Court, 2 Bramber Road,
London W14 9PB, England

www.blake.co.uk

First published in hardback in 2006

ISBN 1 84454 188 6

British Library Cataloguing-in-Publication Data:

A catalogue record for this book is available from the British Library.

Design by www.envydesign.co.uk

Printed in Great Britain by Creative Print & Design, Wales

1 3 5 7 9 10 8 6 4 2

Papers used by John [illegible] clable products made from wood grown in sustainable forests. The manufacturing processes conform to the en[illegible] of the country of origin.

Photographs © page 1 bottom Empics/Michael Sohn, top left Deutschland Polizei/AP/Empics, top right Em[illegible]nfreid Rothermel; page 2 Empics/Uwe Zucchi; page 3 Empics/Douglas Healey; page 4 top Empics, bottom Co[illegible]ghton; page 5 [illegible], Brighton; page 6 top Ron Heflin/AP/Empics, bottom AP/Empics/Matthew Hicks; page 7 Empics/AP Photo/The Dallas Morning News; page 8 Empics/Vincent Yu

In memoriam Jane Longhurst

Contents

INTRODUCTION

'The attraction of the internet to so many people is you can be whoever or whatever you want to be. If you want to be Walter Mitty, you can be Walter Mitty. If you want to be out of the mainstream sexually, you can find company on the internet.'

PAUL JONES, INSTITUTE FOR ADVANCED TECHNOLOGY IN THE HUMANITIES, UNIVERSITY OF VIRGINIA

Cyberspace is a strange place, full of both happy and spine-chilling surprises. And there were certainly some of the second for luckless 28-year-old Trevor Tasker. This Englishman, from North Yorkshire, has understandably given up using the internet since discovering his new love was a 65-year-old pensioner with a corpse in her freezer.

After meeting her in a chatroom, the excited Trevor flew to South Carolina to meet Wynema Faye Shumate, who had posed as a sexy 30-something on the web. After hooking him with sexy chat, she had reeled him in with a semi-nude photo. Unbeknownst to her suitor, however, the shot had been taken some 30 years earlier.

Trevor's shock on first setting eyes on his prospective lover turned to abject horror when he discovered that Wynema had put her dead housemate in the freezer. She had kept Jim O'Neil, who had died of natural causes, in cold storage for a year while she lived in his house and spent his money.

Sweet Wynema had also lopped off one of Jim's legs with an axe because, somewhat inconveniently, he was too big to fit into the freezer. For the record, Shumate pleaded guilty to fraud and the unlawful removal of a dead body, and was given a year in prison.

Back home with his mum afterwards, Trevor told the *Daily Mirror* newspaper, 'I'll never log on again. When I saw her picture, I thought, "Wow", but when she met me at the airport I almost had a heart attack. I certainly won't go near internet chatrooms again.'

Well done, Trevor!

But there is a more serious side to our Introduction.

On 9 March 2004, a chilly Tuesday, the BBC reported that Britain and the USA were setting up a group to investigate ways of closing down internet sites depicting violent sex.

'Initial steps have now been agreed by the Home Secretary David Blunkett and US Deputy Attorney General Jim Comey, during a meeting at the US Department of Justice in Washington DC,' claimed the feature, adding, 'The Jane Longhurst murder case had horrified American officials because websites, featuring extreme sexual acts, were implicated in the trial of Englishman Graham Coutts, who had murdered the Brighton teacher.'

The sexual deviant Coutts trawled the web – there are more than 80,000 sites dedicated to 'snuff' and other killings, cannibalism, necrophilia and rape – then carried out his horrendous fantasy in real life by murdering Jane. The internet-inspired monster kept his victim's body in a garden shed for 11 days, before moving her to a storage facility, where he committed necrophiliac acts on the corpse.

A senior detective from the National Criminal Intelligence Service (NCIS) told Christopher Berry-Dee, who visited New Scotland Yard in 2003, 'In a short period of time, the internet has become the most exploited instrument of perversion known to man. It is like pumping raw sewage into people's homes.'

Also very much to the point is the view of Ron P Hawley, Head of the North Carolina State Bureau of Investigation division which probes computer crimes: 'It used to be you were limited by geography and transportation. The internet broadens the potential for contact. It's another place to hang out for people predisposed to commit a crime.'

In addition to the countless millions of others hooked up to the web, more than a million people now use wireless technology (Wi-Fi) to access it, and a survey found that more than a third of Wi-Fi networks in London and Frankfurt lacked even basic security measures. It's not surprising police throughout the world are increasingly concerned about Wi-Fi cyber crime – particularly the theft of bank details from computers. And some criminals, including paedophiles, are known to leave their networks unprotected so that they can pretend that any illegal activities were not committed by them, attributing the offences instead to 'piggybackers', who log on to the internet via other users' wireless connections.

Another assessment of the internet's potential for crime comes from Yvonne Jukes, of the University of Hull, who claims, with perhaps a little overstatement, 'Cyberspace opens up infinitely new possibilities to the deviant imagination. With access to the internet and sufficient know-how you can, if you are so inclined, buy a bride, cruise gay bars, go on a global shopping spree with someone else's credit card, break into a bank's security system, plan a demonstration in another country and hack into the Pentagon, all on the same day.'

Used with caution, the internet can be an educational and fun place. In fact, most of us have become so reliant on it that we could not conceive of a world without it. At the same time, we're aware of the havoc that can be wrought by viruses on e-commerce when criminals or other hackers attempt to sabotage the web. Indeed, a particularly virulent virus – and more sophisticated forms are being developed all the time – could cause a catastrophe costing billions of dollars – one at least as economically devastating as the 9/11 attack on New York's Twin Towers or Hurricane Katrina's ravaging of New Orleans.

Most people seem to agree that, on balance, the worldwide web has improved our lives. However, among its defenders are those who claim that the advent of the internet, and even the ever-growing availability of virtual pornography, has in no way increased the overall crime figures; least of all that the medium has sparked an escalation in fraud, sexual and violent crime, or murder.

This book sets out to show that these commentators, well

meaning though they may be, could not be more misguided. For the shocking truth is that at no time in human history has crime rocketed to such epidemic proportions over such a short period. A major element in this rise is internet-related crime, which is increasing exponentially, and we can thank thousands of the webmasters hosting sites and search engines for helping things along the way.

To ignore this simple truth is to deny it. Some of us bury our heads in the sand, citing freedom of speech or civil liberties, wishing to demonstrate political correctness or simply concluding, 'Ah well, the web is too powerful now to tackle the problem.' But, if we follow this line of thinking, we will all soon live in a world where anything can happen to us and those appointed to defend our freedoms can do little, if anything, about it.

This brings me back to the well-meaning plans of David Blunkett (the former Home Secretary has since 2004 been succeeded by Charles Clarke) and the US Deputy Attorney General to shut down violent pornography sites. The reality is that, despite a massive UK–US crackdown in recent years, internet child pornography, much of it appallingly violent and degrading, has become a global epidemic of monstrous proportions. In Japan, for instance, Justice Minister Mayami Moryana has said, 'The internet is fuelling a steady increase in child prostitution and pornography. It is a multi-million-dollar child sex trade.'

But this is just one disturbing issue, for US law-enforcement agencies are buckling under the pressure of investigating and bringing to justice *all types* of internet crime-related offences. Funding for police is not finite, nor is manpower. The policing system is creaking, even falling apart, because a large part of these valuable resources is now being diverted to combat well-organised internet crime and lesser offences sparked off by the easy access to the web for the criminally inclined.

Right across Europe and in many parts of Asia, we find a mirror of America's law-enforcement problems, with most countries now admitting almost total defeat in their efforts to curb internet-related crime or closing down sites displaying illegal material. The constant problem is that, as soon as a site is shut down, it reopens under a different domain name. As soon as a problem is located and stopped in one place, it re-emerges somewhere else – often in a more virulent strain – and the perpetrators do not even have to leave their desks to achieve it. In the absence of border controls – cyberspace is by its nature very difficult to police internationally – web-based criminality has become a cyber pandemic.

This is the dilemma now faced by the UK, the USA and other nations; a difficulty compounded in many countries by different interpretations and applications of civil and criminal law and, in the USA, by jurisdictional complications in law enforcement and by civil liberty laws that differ from state to state.

Yet there have been remarkable successes by the multinational task forces set up to catch both those who set up and those who visit child sex sites, and these are down to following the money trails, nearly always through identifying credit-card transactions. But any legislation agreed between the USA and the UK can only apply to sites set up in these countries. And even this is set to be further undermined in the UK as it is due to cede to Brussels much of its own ability to make law and dispense justice, rendering Anglo-American plans to get tough on internet crime all but meaningless.

One major area of crime where the internet's rapid spread has become a highly effective tool is the people-trafficking industry. According to Channel Four's docu-drama *Sex Traffic*, over 50,000 women a year are sold into the USA sex-trafficking trade, and most of the complex logistics are handled using the internet. Trafficking as a whole is growing to such an extent that experts estimate that anywhere from 700,000 to four million persons are now being traded annually throughout the world.

The 'Brides for Sale' business and similar internet scams cost Western males in excess of £4 million a year, and on the subject of this trade George M Nutwell III, Regional Security Officer in the US State Department at the US Embassy in Kiev, has written to the authors, 'Ukraine has recently experienced a burgeoning crop of escort services and "marriage brokers" plying their trade on the internet. Your readers are cautioned against falling into the new Ukrainian "Love Trap".'

A single scam against an Englishman netted a Russian internet dating agency around $11,000 – the staggering, if not obscene equivalent of 25 years' wages for the average Russian citizen. By Western standards, this would be about $500,000. However, the flip side of the coin must not be ignored, for there are hundreds of web pages of advice on how to sensibly approach the task of finding a foreign bride on the internet. Many authorities say that if those seeking a wife are so dumb that they cannot find this advice, or choose to ignore it, they deserve all they get.

To widen the perspective, we now have cyber fraud, theft and just about every other criminal activity, including globally organised terrorism, being promoted and even carried out with the help of the internet. There are some 10,000 websites dedicated to cannibalism and necrophilia. In stomach-turning detail, this book reveals how just one user of such material, Armin Meiwes, made his chilling fantasy come true.

Among the other 'killers on the web' you will meet in these pages is Sol Dos Reis, who is serving a lengthy prison term in the USA for the murder of a young girl he had met after grooming her on the web. Even today he still uses the internet in jail to lure young girls.

All varieties of sex were for sale 24 hours a day in Sharon Lopatka's cyber world. She could provide almost anything anybody desired at any time. The police found it hard to believe that she could willingly board a train with her own murder as her destination. But Sharon wanted to die, and after she met her killer on the internet her wish was granted.

Anastasia Solovyova was a beautiful young woman who travelled from Russia to America to start a happy married life with a man she met on the internet. In a crime that sent shockwaves around the world, she ended up being horrifically abused and brutally murdered.

The sick and twisted John E Robinson became the world's first cyber serial killer, graduating from the personal columns to the internet in search of prey. 'Slavemaster', as he styled himself on the net, kept his victims' bodies in barrels on his remote American smallholding. He has recently been sentenced to death.

Nancy Kissel trawled the internet to seek out information about drugs that she could use to render her husband unconscious before she battered him to death. For his part, it appears, from testimony given by forensic computer experts at his wife's trial in Hong Kong, that Robert Kissel was using the web to search for gay sex.

Susan Gray met an American cyber predator who ran amok in

Britain. He is still at large in the chatrooms and he could be targeting *you*, right now!

The internet also enabled Mona Jaud Awana, a hardline student with links to an Arab terrorist group, to lure a Jewish teenager to his death in Israel. And in an appalling incident in Japan – all the more horrific because it was committed by an 11-year-old child aggrieved by a perceived slight posted on the web – Satomi Mitarai was brutally murdered by her crazed, net-surfing school friend.

Did a knife-wielding maniac attack Darlie Routier in the dead of night? Or had someone else constructed a devilishly intricate plan? It was a crime that shocked America. Now she uses the internet from prison to raise thousands of dollars using deception to further her phoney claims of innocence. In a devastating re-examination of the case, the authors expose a Black Widow of the web.

In fact, hundreds of American male and female prisoners, a few of them serial killers, use the internet to rip off thousands of dollars from gullible sympathisers. Some of the girls post photos of supermodels on the web as a come-on, while others use internet agencies to find pen friends.

It was bound to happen. First, proponents of the culture of death brought us physician-assisted suicide (PAS). Now we must contend with internet-assisted suicide (IAS).

Of course, all of the above we may in some way understand, and there are those who have no objections to any of it. But we are, as a global society, standing on the edge of the cyber abyss, and it is not a matter of if, but simply when, a crazed maniac DVDs a snuff murder and puts it on the web.

In fact, this horrifying reality is already upon us, with obscene, yet professionally shot, footage having been sent down the pipe of the beheadings of Englishman Ken Bigley and US citizens Daniel Pearl, Eugene Armstrong, Jack Kensley, Nicolas Berg, Paul Johnson, among others, as well as horrendous images of the decapitation and shooting dead of a group of Nepalese workers.

Best known among the crazed maniacs responsible for displaying such atrocities is Jordanian militant Abu Musab al-Zarqawi, who uses the internet as a powerful propaganda tool and a means to recruit followers.

Anyone who has viewed these terrifying images cannot fail to be sickened, yet accessing them via any search engine takes moments, and the authors have learned that scores of school children in their early teens have viewed them and boasted to their friends, who in turn have logged on to the sites.

However, the decision as to whether to ban these sites is left to the discretion of the ISPs (internet service providers) and, while a few have made them impossible to view, others make them viewable within seconds.

People being executed, victims of the most horrific homicides, train suicides and many more obscenities – all are readily available to those whose lives are apparently empty of compassion for their fellows; those with little else on their minds but human suffering, and whose minds are readily seeded with images of the worst depravities being committed in the world today.

This book is not just about the offenders who commit internet crime. It also focuses on the web industry, revealing the most shocking facts about who actually sponsors the hosting of porn and crime on the internet.

When you study the facts in these pages, the worldwide web

will never seem the same again. For we turn the spotlight on the real pimps and you will learn that the internet as we know it today would implode if funds from the porn producers dried up.

So, while governments may attempt to outlaw and eradicate websites showing violence and hardcore pornography, ultimately it falls to the morality of the ISPs to decide what is hosted and what is not, and it's here that we find the biggest problem of all.

One of the world's biggest internet companies, Digex, has Microsoft as its largest customer; its second largest customer is the sex industry. The internet industry will not admit to the pervasiveness of pornography on the internet because it profits enormously from pornography in all of its extreme forms.

As an exhibitor at an adult entertainment trade exhibition said, 'The whole internet is being driven by the adult industry. If all this [products at an online prostitution industry trade show] were made illegal tomorrow, the internet would go back to being a bunch of scientists discussing geek stuff in email.'

It may require a Herculean effort, but an international code of conduct is needed to police the internet, with search engines being required to conform rigorously to the agreed standards. It is far easier to close down an international search engine than to nitpick away at individual sites – a time-consuming, costly and ultimately unrewarding exercise.

In truth, the authors are very mindful of the flip side of the coin: these undesirable sites would not exist if millions of visitors did not frequent them and graze on their contents. And because it's a two-way street, these surfers must share responsibility for the sites' existence.

The Internet Watch Foundation says that the world wants the

web and so now we have to live with all of its consequences, like them or not. The genie is out of the bottle and flying about our heads wherever we are on the planet.

One of the few safeguards – and a feeble one it is – is that most pornographic sites contain warnings about their content and the decision as to whether or not to enter them is left to the individual.

The authors' research for this book confirms that a large number of people have become addicted to various types of internet sites and that corresponding types of crime are rising rapidly as a consequence. It proves too that those who harbour thoughts and fantasies of committing such crimes find encouragement and support by logging on.

In the course of this investigation into the internet's grip on the criminal world, and by extension on the lives of all of us, we enter many chilling true-crime nightmares.

Christopher Berry-Dee, 2006

IN THE BEGINNING THERE WAS... JEFF PETERS AND ANDY TAKERS

'Once in a great while, a few times in history, a human mind produces an observation so acute and unexpected that people can't quite decide which is more amazing – the fact or the thinking of it,' wrote Bill Bryson in *A Short History of Nearly Everything*. He was referring to the towering genius of Isaac Newton, but the same observation might equally be applied, if somewhat glibly, to an idea devised by two individuals less principled than the great 17th-century scientist. Our men are the legendary scammers Jeff Peters and his loyal friend the aptly named Andy Takers, who practised their skills in the matrimonial industry long before the advent of the internet.

These two scallywags hit upon a unique idea – it was the first ever in its field, so gullible males stumbled into it in ignorance – and decided to organise a low-risk venture by placing an advertisement in a newspaper aimed at singles. It was simple, and it would make them millionaires: 'Wealthy nice widow is looking for an honest man who will take care of her and her finances. Age and looks are not important but he must have a heart of gold.'

To ensure that the police would not trouble them, Peters and Takers found a real widow. Then they charged every male applicant $50 to have his letter forwarded to 'Widow X'.

Money came pouring in, expenses were covered and the devious venture started to make a profit. Any police officers who knocked on their door were sent away smiling with a small 'bonus' for their concern. Before long, Peters and Takers grew very rich indeed and from the basement of a brownstone in New York they moved swiftly into palatial cliff-top homes, where they were eagerly cosseted by more women than they could count.

Their success is quite amazing when one considers that singles ads had been around for over a century before these two rogues came up with their ingenious get-rich-quick scheme in the early 1940s. But the record also shows that the American serial killers Martha Beck and Raymond Fernandez certainly recognised lonely hearts clubs as a rich source of pickings when, circa 1948, they started to attract their many victims via this medium.

Enticing single and often wealthy women into their net, the couple, dubbed by the press 'the Lonely Hearts Killers', were rewarded for their initiative by electrocution at Sing Sing on 8 March 1951, dying within minutes of each other. It was reported that Martha was so large that special arrangements had to be made for her launch into perdition. She could not fit into the seat, so officers strapped her down while she sat on an arm of the electric chair. An unedifying sight indeed.

Messrs Peters and Takers, Beck and Fernandez might be said

to be the pioneers of 'exploitation for criminal gain' in the lonely hearts end of the sex industry. Such services have been advertised by every medium known to mankind and, above all, on the computer screens now used by most of us.

Indeed, if applause is appropriate, we might say that every rascal who turns a profit from the lonely hearts industry today might put their hands together for Peters and Takers, for without this pair's original idea they would all be a lot poorer. Conversely, their victims would have been richer and, as the case of Robert Wheeler will highlight later in this book, some of them would not have lost their lives.

But let us not forget that the online dating agencies and the lonely hearts clubs before them owe a debt of great magnitude to the person who was the very first to come up with the idea of advertising for a partner. Stand up, Helen Morrison from Manchester!

The short story of Helen Morrison is that of a lonely lady who, way back in 1727, was just looking for a little love. Such was her anguish at being lonely that she persuaded the *Manchester Weekly Journal* to print a tiny notice stating that she was looking for someone nice to share her life with.

Not much wrong with that. But, unfortunately for the lonely spinster, it was not long before this prototype lonely heart ad was reported to the police and Helen was hauled up to face the mayor of Manchester, who quickly had her committed for four weeks to what was then called a lunatic asylum.

History tells us nothing more about Helen. It does, however, show that the early lonely hearts clubs that followed her idea were the ancestors of the millions of websites that offer similar services today.

Understanding this progression from lonely hearts columns to internet dating agencies, to 'Russian Brides Seeking Love', to prostitution and X-rated porn, takes no great leap of the imagination. The original concept has now blossomed into a multi-million-dollar industry – and sex is the root of it all.

You don't have to be a genius to start an internet dating or marriage site. The tools required are simply a website, an e-bank account and Western Union address (which can be used all over the world), and a cluster of pictures of attractive women and men to post on the internet. You link your site to as many others as possible, and you're in business. Fifty or so photos of scantily dressed young females seeking love with older – often much older – men are the best bait around, and you won't have to wait long for the fish to bite.

Most certainly, the priapic Hugh Heffner, owner of *Playboy* magazine, saw the massive potential of the web immediately and was quick to jump in. Making its debut in 1994, *Playboy*'s website had content that differed from the printed version, being designed to appeal to a younger, wealthier audience, 75 per cent of whom did not subscribe to the magazine.

Two years later, the *Playboy* site was the eleventh most visited on the internet. When the magazine *Penthouse* went online in April 1996, its site recorded the highest number of visits for a publication's site on the web – ever.

In 1997, the *Playboy* site generated $2 million in advertising revenue. In mid-1998, *Playboy*'s CyberClub had 26,000 subscribers each paying $60 per year. Today the membership is several million and the site averages a staggering five million hits a day.

By mid-1995, US strip clubs had got in on the act and started setting up websites. From coast to coast, they put up their own pages and used them to advertise their shows. These featured pornographic photographs of strippers and, in imitation of magazine centrefolds, their 'cyberstars' of the week.

A website for a strip club in Delaware pushed the boundaries further by including pornographic images of women engaged in the types of legal prostitution offered at that club, including couch dancing, table dancing, shower shows and dominatrix acts. This initiative took the world by storm and by 2004 the internet offered a choice of 1.3 million strip sites and clubs.

Soon the idea migrated – via the internet, of course – to the UK, Europe and right around the globe. But enough of facts and figures for the moment – more later – for this book concerns itself mainly with the web's links with sex, prostitutes, pimps and murder. And, as for this last kind of crime, it would not be long before someone would have the idea of inviting fellow web surfers to a last supper, as we shall see below.

ARMIN MEIWES: INTERNET CANNIBAL

'It was passable, but a little tough; it would have been better braised… and the wine, a Riesling, was not at all correct, too sweet, lacking body, next time, perhaps, a Pomeral.'

ARMIN MEIWES ON EATING HIS VICTIM'S PENIS

'There are several hundred people with cannibalistic tendencies in Germany alone, and many thousands around the world. Cannibalism has always been around, but the internet reinforces the phenomenon. You can be in contact with the whole world and do this anonymously.'

CRIMINOLOGIST RUDOLF EGG

The internet has highlighted that there are at least one million people who harbour sexualised cannibalistic fantasies. Discussion forums and user groups exist for the exchange of pictures and stories of such fantasies. Users of these services fantasise about eating, or being eaten, by members of their sexually preferred gender. This cannibalistic inclination, known as paraphilia, is one of the most extreme and 'popular' sexual fetishes.

Today cannibals can shop on the internet for someone to consume. And, to judge from the following case, there is no shortage of websites to titillate people who are eager to be killed and eaten.

But one thing is sure: over the coming years there will be no shortage of people for flesh-eating killers to feed on. The cannibal cult followers themselves operate under disguised names or completely phoney identities in the darkest crevices of cyberspace. People such as Laura, who pleads her bona fides in poor English. 'Please don't tell me I'm sick,' she writes. 'It is just a fantasy, but the realism of it turns me on so much.' Or Robert, who cuts very much to the chase: 'I already have a young, pretty, slightly plump married women from Iowa offering herself to be eaten.'

Most of these people are doubtless fantasists, sexual deviants or plain old fruit bats, but their messages are nonetheless ice-cold chilling, because one of these modern-day would-be cannibals and his willing victim have now stepped out of cyberspace, evolving before our eyes from the virtual into the visceral.

It may be hard to digest, but it appears we live in a time of cannibals. The question is, how can such savagery exist in a supposedly sophisticated world?

When Armin Meiwes, a shy, fair-haired man who lived with

his mother, went sailing with his army buddies, he would always make pasta. 'He didn't eat much himself,' remembered Heribert Brinkman, who organised the trips. Meiwes, it seemed, had an appetite for something different, but it was not until March 2001 that dinner was finally served to his satisfaction.

In the tiny central German village of Rotenburg, in the centuries-old farmhouse bequeathed to him by his mother, Meiwes often sat at the kitchen table and dined on steak with pepper sauce, potatoes, sprouts and a glass of red wine. It is not known what the wine was – but eventually the meat would be from a two- rather than a four-legged source.

While Mrs Meiwes was alive, Armin was restrained. Her son was the apple of her eye and she dominated his very core, so that his fantasies remained just that. Her death, in 1999, released the sick side of his soul, which then found the nurture it needed on the internet. But Meiwes was, apparently, no serial killer. Unlike the American Jeffrey Dahmer, who killed 17 men and ate parts of them, or Andrei Chikatilo, who murdered and gorged on as many as 50 men and women in Russia, Meiwes was in search of not so much a victim as a collaborator, but a fellow chef who would provide the principal ingredient.

And into that role stepped 43-year-old Bernd-Jurgen Brandes.

This computer software designer from Berlin had a predilection that was not to everyone's taste: he paid male prostitutes to whip him until he bled. Now, on Sunday, 11 March 2001, he relaxed in the large comfortable chair offered to him by Meiwes, and sipped from a tumbler of cognac. A contented half-smile played across his host's lips, for this was the moment Armin had been waiting for. He had prepared meticulously for what was now, finally, starting to unfold.

Brandes had written his will and had it notarised. The bulk of his estate, including a sprawling, luxury penthouse apartment, along with a small fortune in computer equipment, had been bequeathed to Rene, his blithely unaware male partner. And he had sold most of his belongings, including an expensive sports car. He wouldn't be requiring these material trappings where he was going.

His wish was to be butchered, cooked and eaten.

Something else Rene could not have suspected was that, when Bernd had informed his bosses at Siemens that he was taking the Friday off 'to attend to some personal matters', he would not be coming back.

With several thousand dollars in cash and his passport tucked inside his jacket, Bernd travelled 300 kilometres from Berlin to the farmhouse near Kassel where he now sat with his drink. His pulse raced, while the warm cognac slowly dulled his senses. He smiled contentedly, knowing he had been very methodical indeed.

Armin Meiwes, the gentleman whom he had first met through the internet some months before and who now stood, beaming broadly in front of him, had been methodical too. Calling himself 'Frankie', he had patiently posted more than 80 notices on a gay internet chatroom with cannibalism as its central theme, waiting calmly for just the right individual to reply. When Bernd, who styled himself 'Cator', finally answered, both men quickly realised that their mutual fantasy would become something much more. After all, it is without question that both parties knew what the other wanted, and this was confirmed in a video recording that captured every sickening moment.

Meiwes had been fishing – trawling might be a more apt term – and on cannibal fetish websites he had encountered a handful of willing participants who took the bait, swam into the net by visiting his home to admire his newly constructed cage and slaughter room, then allowed him to draw lines on their bodies to illustrate the choicest cuts and even let themselves be suspended upside down by a chain and pulley.

Meiwes's culinary plans didn't come to fruition with any of these candidates, but he was a patient fellow. It was not until early 2001 that his message, 'Searching for a well-built young man who would like to be eaten by me', was greeted by: 'I am offering myself to be eaten but alive. No slaughter but consumption.'

Who would reply favourably to an invitation like 'Gay male seeks hunks 18–30 to slaughter', unless that nightmarish sentiment stirred something deep and secret within?

From the start secure within the confines of the rambling half-timbered house so painstakingly customised by his host, Bernd placed his glass on the table beside him and rose. Smiling, he embraced the tall man standing before him and allowed himself to be led out of the room and along a narrow hallway. Once in Meiwes's bedroom, he lay down on the bed and, with that same vapid smile on his face, he observed as the 41-year-old man produced something sharp that gleamed in the lamplight.

Bernd closed his eyes and waited.

First he felt his fly being unzipped and then his slacks slowly being tugged off. Meiwes was gentle but firm, wary of doing anything that might spoil the coming moment. Bernd snapped at him, 'Just do it. Just cut the thing off!' Taking Bernd's flaccid penis in his hand, Meiwes drew the razor-sharp blade slowly across the member several times until it separated from his guest's body.

The pain must have been excruciating and the flow of blood powerful, but this Meiwes partly staunched with a wet towel. Without immediate medical assistance, Bernd would bleed to death, but death is exactly what he wanted.

Both men were unable to consume the penis raw and, unfortunately, when Meiwes tried to cook it, he burned it black.

With Bernd bleeding heavily from his mutilated groin and his time running out, the two men agreed to forgo the first course and head directly for the main dish. With a glass of wine in one hand, the guest proffered the 'delicacy' to his host. Meiwes gladly accepted and, as Bernd looked on, he savoured the heady sensation of realising this powerful mutual fantasy, then took up his knife and fork.

In the yellowy light of the dining room, the delighted castrator tucked into this most succulent, although overdone piece of flesh, savouring it as one might a tender venison steak. He had taken the liberty of frying the organ in garlic butter – he had trusted his guest had no objections. Then, after voicing his approval, he gestured for Bernd to join him and both tucked in.

After dinner, Meiwes waved away his guest's polite offer to help him clear the table. He invited him instead to sit down and make himself comfortable with another cognac. Before long, the two men repaired again to the bedroom, where, after saying goodbye to the almost unconscious Bernd, the gracious host took one last longing glance at the crudely cauterised, gaping, bloody hole between his new friend's legs.

It took many hours for the man to die, during which time

Meiwes read a *Star Trek* novel before setting to work with the sharpest of his butcher knives.

Meiwes had a video camera rolling at the time. He had decided early on in the proceedings that he would allow himself the opportunity to relive this moment time and again. Similarly, Bernd's willing emasculation, followed by the unforgettable meal, was captured for posterity.

After Meiwes had finished plunging his knife into his guest's throat he picked up his video camera and dragged the bloody corpse into his special room. It was here, after he had suspended the body from a meat hook, that the next phase of the ritual began.

At peace in his self-constructed abattoir, surrounded by heavy metal hooks and drains, Meiwes opened the body from groin to sternum and gutted it as one would a deer. Throughout the night he laboured, hacking and severing until finally, one dismembered corpse later, it was time to separate the choicer fleshy morsels and render them into what he would later describe as 'meal-sized packets'.

With his special food supply placed, along with the dead man's skull, in his freezer, he disposed of the cumbersome bones and teeth – and let us not forget the innards – by burying them in the garden.

Meiwes would consume a piece of his friend almost every day, but he never finished the task, for frozen chunks of Bernd-Jurgen Brandes were discovered in his home on his capture on 10 December 2002. Indeed, the crime only came to light when Meiwes, having chewed through 20 kilograms of his victim, began to search for another dish on the internet and a correspondent invited to become a meal took fright.

After being tipped off by worried internet chatroom users about the existence of disturbing advertisements placed by Meiwes, undercover police officers posing as respondents quickly determined that the ads were meant literally. When Meiwes was eventually arrested, his reaction was one of confusion. Why was he being taken away? No crime had been committed. He contested it had all been completely consensual. A congenial arrangement for their mutual pleasure: victim and killer, in it together. The cops, however, took a somewhat different perspective, and the protesting Meiwes was promptly marched off to the police station.

From the very start of his sensational trial, which opened in Kassel on a suitably overcast day, Wednesday, 3 December 2003, Meiwes's primary objective, with the aid of his solicitors, was to convince the jury that he was not a murderer. This they ultimately achieved. The prosecution struggled laboriously to secure dual convictions pertaining to 'sexual murder' and 'disturbing the peace of the dead'. But the fact that videotaped evidence showed beyond a shadow of a doubt that Brandes had been perfectly happy to have his peace disturbed after his demise did not help their case one bit.

After taking in the evidence that the victim had been a willing participant in his own killing, the court was shown the videotape. The pair had clearly been in agreement about filming the killing and the subsequent butchering.

Brandes was seen explaining that, for him, being eaten would be the fulfilment of a dream. As the carnage began, the video revealed two men locked into a very private world.

One of those viewing the grisly film, which also showed

Meiwes talking to the severed head while he disembowelled the body, actually fainted.

The court heard that the killing had taken place in March 2001. Brandes had been reported missing at this time. The judges heard how, for the defendant, the act of eating another human being was akin to the merging of two souls. It was the nearest feeling Meiwes could experience to being close to another person.

At the trial, and with considerable understatement, both Meiwes and Brandes were described as 'having mental difficulties', and Meiwes did little to dissuade psychologists from persisting in this notion. For he disclosed in detail how he had achieved his closeness with Brandes by eating pieces of him for more than a year, and stated that by so doing he had gained the dead man's ability to speak English.

On the topic of the unique dinner, the defendant had an important culinary message to impart. After first trying, unsuccessfully, to bite off Brandes's penis – at his request – he decided that it should be severed with a knife. The freshly removed organ was then sauteed and flambeed, and prepared to be served. Meiwes, with a touch of Hannibal Lecter's panache, delivered his verdict on the dish: 'It was passable, but a little tough; it would have been better braised,' and he paused before adding, 'And the wine, a Riesling, was not at all correct, too sweet, lacking body, next time, perhaps, a Pomeral.'

Later, with the slaughtered Brandes in pieces in his freezer, Meiwes positively revelled in dining every day on this special meat. Retrospectively, the self-confessed connoisseur of human flesh commented, 'Honestly, I've taken a fancy to American-style cuts rather than traditional German or French.'

A brief background of the defendant was supplied by the usual gamut of family, friends and neighbours, who described the killer as pleasant and mild-mannered, a mostly quiet man who kept himself to himself.

He had served a dozen years in the German Army as a non-commissioned ordnance officer and was said to have been an amiable and conscientious military man. After leaving the armed forces in 1991, Meiwes retrained as a computer technician and started working for a software company in the Rhine Valley city of Karlsruhe.

Evoking vividly the shades of Norman Bates from Hitchcock's *Psycho*, Meiwes had lived with his mother in the farmhouse and remained there for several years after her death. One neighbour had put it succinctly for reporters: 'He was a mama's boy.' The young Meiwes had been totally fixated with his overbearing mother, who had never let him have a girlfriend. Meiwes, who in any case preferred boys, had meekly acquiesced. He himself later recounted how his desire to eat another man had begun during puberty and that his fantasy had become so powerful over the years that he always knew he would one day enact it.

Had Meiwes been convicted of murder he would most likely have ended up spending the rest of his life in prison. Considering the ghastly acts involved, justice would surely have demanded no less. Instead, after adhering more to Meiwes's solicitor's claim that his client had merely assisted in a suicide, a panel of judges decided to convict the cannibal of manslaughter: he was sentenced to eight and a half years in jail.

The sentence equates to just over two years for every ten pounds of Bernd-Jurgen Brandes that Meiwes cooked and ate.

Though the court rejected the defence solicitor's main argument, that Meiwes should be convicted of 'killing on request', a form of illegal euthanasia carrying a shorter sentence of six months to five years, it was agreed that he could not be found guilty of murder.

Judge Volker Muetze, one of those presiding at the trial, said the deed was 'viewed with revulsion in our civilised society', but, on the basis of the very clear video evidence presented, Meiwes had not committed murder, the hushed courtroom was informed. Instead, he had displayed 'a behaviour which is condemned in our society, namely the killing and butchering of a human being. Seen legally, this is manslaughter, killing a person without being a murderer'.

As the verdict was read, Meiwes maintained the same relaxed posture he had throughout the two-month trial, where he had earlier been given the opportunity to question witnesses against him. This he had done in a most precise and unemotional manner.

Meiwes had been waiting for many years for an opportunity to realise his gruesome fantasies. With the advent of the internet he seized his chance. Taking full advantage of the medium's success as a huge dating agency, he was able to cast his net for prospective candidates. It transpired that Meiwes had 'auditioned' four other potential victims who had agreed to be examined for physical suitability by the prospective killer.

Hooked by internet ads proclaiming lurid offers like 'I could just gobble you up' and 'Let me feast on you', these four individuals – three from Germany and one from London – travelled separately to Meiwes's house for their interview and examination. Three of the men baulked when faced with the reality of being cannibalised, having initially assumed it was all part of some erotic role-playing game. The fourth was rejected as 'pudgy and unsexy' by the very particular Meiwes.

Continuing to trawl the internet in search of the perfect human meal, Meiwes eventually stumbled across his main course.

After his trial and sentencing, it was observed by many eminent authorities that on his release – possibly as early as 2008 – it is unlikely that he will become a repeat offender. One expert on cannibalism, an author named Jacques Buval, felt slightly differently about the matter: 'Cannibalism is like paedophilia. It is in him. You can't cure it. He will want to do it again.'

Judge Muetze made this disturbing observation: 'We have learned through this process that there is a massive cannibal following out there [on the internet].' So how many other ghouls like Armin Meiwes are presently at work, flourishing as a result of the ease of ensnaring their prey over the internet? Dozens, hundreds, thousands?

Research has shown that there are an estimated 10,000 cannibal websites, with millions of equally lonely people who sit for hours and hours in front of their computer screens, fantasising about eating someone – perhaps *you*!

The Meiwes case has opened the door on something far more insidious and pernicious: the secret world of the suburban cannibal, and the internet is the key.

The four men who met Meiwes before he killed Brandes were clearly prepared to indulge in a deep and dark sexual fantasy, part bondage and part flagellation. They allowed him to wrap them up in cellophane and mark out their body parts as joints of meat. When they chickened out, Meiwes let them go.

Countless websites dedicated to cannibalism and portraying horrific photographs of women apparently being prepared for eating by roasting and boiling alive are linked to hard-porn sites.

Are the Western world's eating habits changing, or what?

SAUL DOS REIS: OUTSIDER

'I have many qualities which make me unique. I'm romantic, always funny, I always have a positive attitude and have many hidden things as well.'

SAUL DOS REIS AS HE ADVERTISED FOR PEN FRIENDS ON THE WEB FROM JAIL

Twenty-five million Americans visit cyber sex sites for between one and ten hours a week, while another 4.7 million log on for in excess of 11 hours per week. And when Saul Dos Reis, a 24-year-old Brazilian national living in Greenwich, Connecticut, lured 13-year-old Christina Long to her death, he used the internet to help him.

On 17 May 2002, Dos Reis would meet the pretty, golden-haired schoolgirl. Before he left her that night, he had raped and strangled her.

Dos Reis looked anything but threatening. One has only to glimpse this man, who appears to be more like a boy, to form this opinion. A slender-faced, shy-looking fellow, he looks as though he would be more at home delivering the local paper, smiling meekly if ever he earned himself a tip. But Saul was a wolf in sheep's clothing; seemingly charming, even bookish, yet simmering with anger at the all-American girls because he resented the stigma that he felt came with his Brazilian heritage here in the United States. Quite wrongly, he perceived himself to be a second-class citizen. He had low self-esteem and, although not unattractive to the opposite sex, he felt that he was unable to form a meaningful relationship with a girl in the face of the competition from his thoroughbred American peers.

As he grew older, this view of himself as someone different – someone who couldn't even speak English when he came to America, so had no chance of chatting to the desirable girls he would see on the school bus – remained with him long enough for Saul to develop a serious grudge against young white females. And, as he would quickly discover after arriving in New England's 'Nutmeg State', Connecticut was anything but the Land of the Free.

Saul had first set foot on North American soil as a ten-year-old immigrant. This thin, outwardly unassuming boy with thick, dark hair and coffee-coloured skin would learn fast that girls in the United States could be quite selective as to whom they spent their time with. This seemed to him to be a pervasive attitude and the impressionable young outcast, in his strange new land, did not care for it one bit.

He festered, withdrawing into a dark world of bitterness and frustration, to become a brooding, sullen loner. Young Saul, with South America in his blood, had felt very much out of place when his family first came to Fairfield County. In Greenwich, with its 60,000 residents, he was not only a long way from home but also felt all the more isolated as he was part of the mere 1.4 per cent of the town's population that was of Hispanic origin.

In conservative Connecticut, pleasant beaches and rolling hills share the land with bustling cities and seafront casinos; it seems there is something for everybody. With such scenic treasures as Litchfield Hills, Housatonic River and Connecticut River Valley, the state also boasts a variety of parks, quaint village greens and hiking and biking trails. It also has its fair share of deep ravines. If a body were tossed into one of these it could be some time before anybody would find it.

Locked away in his small bedroom, Saul Dos Reis spent hundreds of hours on his computer. Soon he had gained a lot of experience of using chatrooms to ensnare underage girls. In cyberspace he could reinvent himself. He could become anyone he so chose.

Enchanted by the masses of syrupy dialogue spewing forth from him, impressionable teenage girls were very keen to engage with the young and pleasant-looking Dos Reis, who, if they were lucky, would send a photograph of himself. Of infinitely greater importance to the man on the other end of the modem, they would send through a picture of *them*selves.

He would pore over these images, fantasising about all the things he could do to an attractive, all-American teenage girl. The pictures the girls sent in return only added more excitement to the anticipatory conversations they had shared online.

In 1998, Dos Reis had met a 15-year-old-girl from nearby

Prospect with whom he had built a shadowy relationship in a chatroom. The girl consented to intercourse with the tightly wound internet Casanova and, for reasons unknown, she was not harmed. Four years and countless obsessive chatroom babblings later, Christina Long would not be so fortunate.

Pictures of Christina show a truly lovely young girl. Facing the camera, she is not bashful but smiles happily, her pretty features framed by her flowing golden-brown hair. To Dos Reis, she was a delightful-looking creature, poised and full of life. At her Catholic school, where she was a sixth-grader, Christina was a good student. As well as heading the cheerleading squad she was an altar girl.

'I'm so devastated,' said Andrea Cappiello, Christina's one-time fifth-grade English and religious education teacher, when asked to comment on the sad death of her former pupil. 'She was a very good student and a very good cheerleader. She was very spirited, just a doll.' But the girl also evidenced a harder side. 'She was streetwise,' Andrea said. 'But you could see the other side coming up, too. It's clear she was very torn in both directions.'

For Christina was not without her problems.

After striking up some online conversations – chats which became increasingly sexually overt – the ostensibly all-American girl began to fall for the worldly-seeming allure of Dos Reis. For example, apparently referring to a Lexus car, he used the screen name 'Hot es300' for the model. Obviously, his intention was to convey smoothness. And along with this came a barrage of lewd dialogue. As Danbury Police Chief Robert Paquette later revealed, 'There was some pretty graphic stuff [in the chatroom logs].'

Indeed, Christina was no stranger to sexual encounters with

partners she had met over the internet. She had become absorbed in an ultimately destructive pattern of dating boys she had conversed with online. And sex was something she was more than prepared to engage in with her 'boyfriends'.

She had come to the town of Danbury two years previously to live with her aunt, Shelly Riling, because her parents were heavy drug users. Riling, very concerned about her niece's welfare, was eventually awarded custody of the girl. She apparently didn't know anything about Christina's online activities, although she had had to speak to her more than once about the late nights she sometimes kept.

Over the next several weeks, Dos Reis was finally able to persuade Christina to meet him. The two had several sexual encounters before their fateful rendezvous at the Danbury Fair Mall, and their final fatal date took place in the back seat of Saul's car.

As Dos Reis is the last man to have seen Christina alive, we must rely on his word as to what occurred in the events leading to her murder. It is doubtful that the version offered by this rapist and strangler of a young girl has any real mooring in truth, but it is nonetheless instructive when exploring the mindset of a sexual criminal and his rationalisations.

Dos Reis later insisted to police that not only had Christina wanted sex but also that she had requested 'rough sex'. Unfortunately, this had been taken a little too far and she had somehow accidentally ended up strangled and dead. If Dos Reis expects us to believe that in the throes of passion he had inadvertently choked his young partner, let us note that it takes around five minutes to strangle somebody to death.

Allegedly panicked by this sudden surge of violence, the

young man drove to a remote ravine, where he dumped Christina's body.

Not long afterwards, when the police had linked him via an email indicating that he had agreed to meet Christina on the Friday night, Dos Reis immediately caved in and told them his story. With the FBI involved, it was at their insistence that he led them to Christina's violated corpse. He displayed not a trace of the bravado that had been the staple of his relationships with his 'girls'. Rather, like a naughty puppy, he hung his head in shame. It seemed that his days of surfing the net for young teens were over. As it later transpired, this wasn't the case.

Dos Reis was later arraigned in the US District Court in Bridgeport on a charge of using an interstate device – the internet – to entice a child into sexual activity. He was ordered held without bond, with a bail hearing scheduled for later that week.

At his trial in Bridgeport, which lasted from Monday, 3 March to Monday, 7 July 2003, he pleaded guilty to manslaughter and three counts of second-degree sexual assault.

Sniffling and speaking so softly that the judge had repeatedly to ask him to speak up, Dos Reis, now 25, apologised for killing Christina Long. 'I have not had a single night of sleep when I don't wake up drenched in sweat,' he said.

Presiding Judge Patrick L Carroll III said the apology should have come sooner. 'That time for mercy was the evening your victim died at your hands,' he admonished the defendant.

During the 'victim impact' phase of the case, and before handing down the maximum sentence allowable for the crimes, Judge Carroll heard several tear-filled statements from members of both Dos Reis's and Christina's families.

Christina's grandfather, Lawrence Long, held nothing back,

calling Dos Reis a 'habitual predator' who used his computer, flashy car, money and previous life experiences to lure Christina to her death. Dos Reis's supporters presented an entirely different picture, testifying as to how he had provided free meals to the needy at his father-in-law's restaurant. When his father-in-law's wife had cancer, Dos Reis cared for her and even shaved his own head to make her feel more comfortable while she underwent chemotherapy.

After listening attentively to both sides, the judge handed down what he could: 30 years in a state prison on manslaughter and sexual assault charges. It was also made known that in September of the previous year Dos Reis had received a 25-year federal sentence on two charges of travelling in interstate commerce to engage in illegal sex with a minor.

Ten years of the federal sentence was to be served consecutively with the state sentence – a total of 40 years behind bars.

There was one niggling issue, however, and that was whether or not US District Court Judge Stefan Underhill was unreasonable in the matter of Dos Reis's sentencing, when he handed down a term that did not quite adhere to the usual sentencing guidelines. Under these guidelines Dos Reis's offences would have called for a sentence of a little more than seven years.

Later, in the Second Circuit US Court of Appeals, James Lenihan, Dos Reis's lawyer, argued that the sentence was 'unlawful' and should be sent back to the District Court to be 'substantiated'.

Lenihan also said that the District Court 'mistakenly noted that age was a factor to be considered' under the guidelines, but in fact the guidelines did not make reference to the victim's age.

Although Christina's death was not an element of the federal charge, the federal judge took the killing into consideration during the penalty phase. Kevin O'Connor, the state attorney for Connecticut, argued that Judge Underhill did not make a legal error. O'Connor said the departure was justified because the defendant 'knowingly risked the life of his victim when he choked her'. He said the sentence was reasonable 'in light of the horrific circumstances of the defendant's strangulation of Christina, dumping of her dead body, and efforts to cover up his involvement'.

Christina's death received national attention and sparked a push in Congress for a kids-only domain on the internet. On 27 May 2003, it was announced that legislation allowing Connecticut Police to more swiftly investigate internet sex crimes like the one that led to the death of Christina Long had failed because state lawmakers were concerned about violating civil liberties.

So, while officials praised the quickness of the FBI in tracking down Dos Reis, state experts and local police felt that Connecticut's reliance on federal agencies was unwise, given the rapid spread of internet sex crime. 'Everybody has their own job to do,' said Danbury Detective Captain Mitchell Weston, 'and we were lucky in this case that the FBI wasn't in the middle of something.'

It seemed unlikely that the killing could have been prevented. FBI spokeswoman Lisa Bull said the FBI learned of previous contact between the girl and the older Dos Reis only during the investigation into her killing.

Laws proposed in the General Assembly would have helped track down the perpetrators in cases where police have knowledge of illegal internet contact between adults and children. The bureau – comprising only state police – responsible for dealing with internet crime have written bills empowering state authorities to more easily obtain internet users' identities and communications logs.

These bills would, in theory, have encompassed not only the use of internet messages to lure someone to a potentially indecent encounter, but also the murkier depths of the provision of indecent imagery of children. Unfortunately, they did not survive the legislative committee process.

Griswold's Democrat representative, Steven Mikutel, a co-sponsor of one of the bills, said the Legislature did not have the political will to make it law. 'There is a group out there that doesn't want to put any restrictions on the internet,' he said, adding, 'They don't want to invade anyone's privacy. But public safety factors have to come into consideration here.'

Danbury Police Chief Robert Paquette offered this: 'You're getting into civil liberties now. I don't think either the federal government or the state can go that far.'

Later, another man who had had sex with the clearly underage Christina was put out of commission. On 15 March 2004, 24-year-old Carlos Estanqueiro, also a former resident of Danbury, was sentenced to 46 months for the offence. He had pleaded guilty the previous December to using the internet for the purposes of 'persuading a minor to engage in sex'.

Estanqueiro, it materialised, had met Christina over the internet in February 2002. The pair had subsequently engaged in sexual activities several times.

New Haven US District Judge Janet B Arterton ensured that, in addition to the prison time Estanqueiro would serve, there would be a further three years of supervised release. It was further stipulated that Estanqueiro register as a convicted sex offender on his release. Arterton also ordered that he undergo mental-health counselling, not frequent locations where children are known to congregate and not use a computer except for work-related purposes. Estanqueiro was also an illegal alien. As such, he could be subject to deportation after serving his time.

The battle to protect children from internet stalkers continues. On one website visited by the authors, it is clear that help is available:

'The freedom that makes the internet so useful also makes it dangerous. In teen chatrooms, sexual predators can hunt for their victims online, 24 hours a day,' it warns. The existence of links such as 'Wise up to Internet Predators', 'Protecting Kids From Internet Porn' and 'Children, Sex and the Web' makes it clear that at least we are on the right track.

A lawyer and expert in the field of internet abuse, Parry Aftab, says, 'Internet predators attempt to lure thousands of children every year to offline meetings.'

These are her guidelines:

Who's at risk?

What's the profile of an internet child molester?

How often does this happen?

Why do the children meet strangers offline?

What can you do to protect your children?

What's being done to find these predators before they hurt a child?

Whom do you call if you suspect someone is involved with targeting children online?

A survey of 10,800 teenage girls conducted in 1998 showed that 12 per cent of the sample admitted to meeting up with strangers with whom they had first made contact via the internet. Two years later, *Family PC* reported that, in a survey of both sexes, 24 per cent of the teenage girls polled and 14 per cent of the teenage boys were meeting internet strangers offline.

It is truly a shame that Christina Long did not benefit from the various safety precautions now available on the internet. It took her death, among so many others, to bring home to us the dangers of the internet. Had her online activities been more closely monitored through this kind of education, she may never have had the opportunity to come into contact with her dysfunctional killer. Dos Reis was then, and in all likelihood still is, a very dangerous man.

As an obscene postscript to this terrible crime, it was recently discovered that Dos Reis was up to his old tricks again, this time inside prison. In search of female correspondents, he had set up a web page, although this now appears to have been removed. He included a photograph of himself, this time smiling and sporting a tuxedo. Above the ad he had selected the heading 'The Right One'.

On his web page, Dos Reis went on to describe his perfect penpal as 'A woman with a good heart that loves to write and that is not afraid of being herself', adding, 'I also look for a person that knows what she wants out of life.'

His readers could learn that: 'I have many qualities which make me unique. I'm romantic, always funny, I always have a positive attitude and have many hidden things as well. I enjoy writing and being silly and funny' and 'I also always carry on interesting things to talk about. I'm not just another boring penpal…'

He decided to inform his prospective lonely hearts that he had been convicted of second-degree assault. So, with just a slight deviation from the truth yet again, the 'Outgoing Heterosexual Male' made it apparent that he 'prefers female correspondents but will reply to all letters'. He also claimed to be 'very good at telling stories which can and will have you shiver'.

Christina's aunt, Shelly Riling, was shocked by the web page, denouncing it as a prime example of 'predatory behaviour'. However, Dos Reis's defence attorney, Peter Tilem, argued that his client's web page is understandable. 'This is someone who is going to spend the next 30 years in prison and he's lonely and scared,' he said. 'We can't imagine how lonely he feels, so I can understand.'

According to inmate.com, prisoners can place an ad for four months for $60 and $15 for each subsequent month. The website designs and posts the ad for the subscriber. Purchasers of premium advertisements, such as Dos Reis, are given a personal email box that allows people to respond to the ad via email. Once a week the service forwards the email responses to the inmate in a letter. And what a nice little earner this is for the site's owners. For seed money outlay, they rake in $37,000 a year by making it possible for people such as Dos Reis to involve other people in their sickening fantasies from behind bars.

Christina's aunt did not share Tilem's assessment. 'I can't believe he has a website. It shows that he has a disease and is incurable. He hasn't learned anything.'

Investigators involved with the Dos Reis case were at a loss to find a motive for the murder. Indeed, even the killer himself was unable to cast much light on his reason for strangling the young woman. However, we know from experience that many people who spend long periods of time in chatrooms become of another world. Susan Gray, discussed later in this book, is a graphic example of the phenomenon.

These individuals find themselves becoming addicted to the chatrooms and perceive themselves as engaging in very real relationships with other visitors. They are people who have in most cases reinvented themselves to compensate for their own psychological and/or physical shortcomings. For those addicted to the chatrooms, it becomes a meeting of 'loners' who bring all of their psychological inadequacies along with them.

These people actually fall in 'cyber love' – in much the same way as couples do in the real world. Saul Dos Reis seems, for whatever reason, to have fallen in love with Christina Long in this way. He had become 'fantasy-driven'. After years of rejection, he imagined he had found his ideal partner, even though she was underage. Christina was promiscuous and her sexual appetite, coupled with her pretty looks, no doubt further increased his need for her companionship. Nevertheless, after she had had sex with him a few times, the feisty girl wanted to dump him and move on. Rejected, and scorned again, Dos Reis killed her.

This scenario of a cyber *crime passionnel* is not quite as crazy as it first appears, as the following cases testify.

On 15 February 2004, a man was found trying to commit suicide at his home in Wuhan, China. Afterwards, he admitted that he had killed his cyber lover on Valentine's Day evening.

The man, using the net name 'Flying Dust', got to know 'Rain Drop', a 25-year-old flower-shop keeper, at the end of 2003. They met in a chatroom, but Rain Drop's parents disapproved of her having such an intimate online relationship. So, on Valentine's Day, she told Flying Dust that she had to break up with him. He flew into a rage and strangled her to death, and then tried to cut the arteries on his neck and wrists. 'I love her, I want to be with her for ever,' he said later, when asked why he had done it.

On Saturday, 17 April 2004, a man's body was found in a hotel room in Dengshikou, Beijing. Zhang Yang had been killed by his cyber lover, Liang Yixia, because he refused to marry her. Liang was arrested when she came back to get her mobile phone charger.

According to Liang, in May 2003 she had been raped by three men she met on the internet, and they also took her money. After her ordeal, Zhang, a seemingly gentle and rich man, renewed her trust in cyber love. But, once they had had sex, he told her that for him to marry a cyber lover was impossible. Liang felt so humiliated that she fed him sleeping pills before strangling him with adhesive tape.

At the police station, Liang said she felt no regret for what she had done. 'He deserved this punishment I gave him,' she said repeatedly.

In 2001, a West Australian Supreme Court jury found a woman guilty of murdering her internet lover, after he tried to dump her when he discovered that she was married to a biker. The woman was caught on the home-security video of the man she murdered and is now serving a mandatory life sentence for the crime.

Thirty-four-year-old Margaret Hinchcliffe met Michael Ian Wright, aged 30, in an internet chatroom and the two soon began a sexual relationship. In November 1999, Hinchcliffe's husband, Mark, found out about the affair and inflicted a series of punishments on his wife, driving her to seek help at a women's refuge on two occasions. A worker from the refuge told the court that Margaret had been badly beaten by her husband and that he had ordered her to shave her head. He also ordered her to have a tattoo done on her waistline that read 'Property of Mark Hinchcliffe'.

Mark Hinchcliffe, a member of a bikers' gang who called themselves the Coffin Cheaters' Club, visited Wright and threatened him after beating him up. He then ordered his wife to kill Wright, an order she carried out on Sunday, 25 February 2000.

Margaret Hinchcliffe went to the home of Wright's parents, and when Wright opened the door she shot him at point-blank range, unaware of the fact that the video security system had captured the act on film.

In Columbus, Ohio, Rickie Mandes slipped his old .45-calibre handgun into his pocket before taking one last moment in his lonely apartment to think about his two daughters. Within a few hours, those two girls, aged nine and 15, would be fatherless. Their lives would be shaken by a nightmare of violence, jealousy and revenge. Mandes would be dead, and so would Robert J Fry, the man he believed had stolen his wife's affection over the internet.

Mandes felt his daughters needed some kind of explanation. And so, in a hastily scrawled note to them, he tried to provide one, writing that the pain and stress he felt after his wife, Rebecca, had left him for a man she had met over the internet was 'too much for me to take. I am sorry for what I am about to do.'

Authorities said the 45-year-old Mandes confronted his wife and her new lover in the parking lot of the mail-order store where Fry worked and gunned him down, then turned the weapon on himself.

Acquaintances of the Mandeses, who had known the couple in happier days, closed ranks and have refused to discuss the events that led to the brutal murder and suicide. 'They want their privacy,' said long-time friend Tammy Campbell of the surviving members of the family.

According to police, the slaying was sparked by an internet romance that had blossomed over two and half months between 34-year-old Rebecca Mandes and 40-year-old Fry.

A little more than a month and a half after the whirlwind online romance began, Fry suddenly quit his job of 22 years at the Orient Correctional Facility in Ohio. He left his wife and children, and moved with Rebecca Mandes and her two girls into a house in the pleasant waterfront community of Westerly. Two weeks before the shooting, he took a job in the receiving department of Paragon Gifts store.

By all accounts, Rebecca's decision to move out of the apartment she and her husband shared in Pawcatuck was equally abrupt.

There were a few domestic loose ends to be tied up, which provided Mandes with the opportunity he needed to exact his revenge on the man he believed had stolen his wife, so he and his wife had arranged to meet in the parking lot of Paragon Gifts about noon to exchange some items belonging to the daughters.

For a while they stood just outside the office window of Paragon Gifts' president Stephen Rowley, waiting for Fry to leave work for his lunch break. About a dozen employees were milling about, and a little after 12.30pm Fry approached the pair.

With that, witnesses told police, Mandes pulled out the gun, said something to the effect of 'This is what you get for messing with my wife' and opened fire.

Stephen Rowley heard 'what I'd call a pop, several of them close together', he said. 'Then there was a moment of silence, and another pop,' which he later learned was the sound of the final bullet that crashed into Mandes's skull, killing the jilted husband instantly.

Rebecca Mandes was not injured in the attack.

The broken-hearted man had left a short suicide note, simply saying, 'I guess she's doing all right.'

JANE LONGHURST: VICTIM OF A NECROPHILIAC

'In seeking perverted sexual gratification by way of your sordid and evil fantasies, you have taken her life and devastated the lives of those she loved and of those who loved her.'

JUDGE RICHARD BROWN TO GRAHAM COUTTS

'The case of Jane Longhurst and her killer, Graham Coutts, may become a landmark issue that could – if there is the political will – have far-reaching consequences on the future of violent pornography sites in the years to come.'

CHRISTOPHER BERRY-DEE

When Jane Longhurst, a 31-year-old special-needs teacher from the English seaside town of Brighton, vanished without a trace on Friday, 14 March 2003, it was immediately flagged as suspicious. This conscientious, caring young woman would not just up and leave without telling anybody.

Originally from Reading, Jane had moved to the Sussex coast, where, in addition to her teaching, she was a skilled viola player in a local orchestra. She was a bubbly lady with chestnut hair and an effervescent smile. There was a gentle aura surrounding Jane which everyone she came into contact with would attest to.

Jane was described as stable, reliable and dependable and, when suddenly she wasn't there any more, people took notice. There was no word to her family, friends or her employers. And what of the kids with learning disabilities at Uplands School, who were very close to Jane and relied on the kind and patient teacher to help them with their studies?

No one knew where Jane was; she had vanished into thin air.

The one person who realised straight away that something strange, possibly bad, had happened to Jane was her boyfriend, Malcolm Sentance. Very early on, Malcolm was extremely upset by her disappearance. The couple were extremely close and Malcolm had given her a warm hug and goodbye kiss as he left for work, at about 6.45 that morning, from their home in Shaftesbury Road, Brighton.

This was a routine the two followed each day: they would wake up, complete their morning rituals and bid their goodbyes as they set off for the day. It is what many of us do each morning, comfortable in the knowledge that all is well and that we will be seeing our loved one as usual later that evening.

Sometimes, though, terrible things occur, and they can

happen to anyone. Often the first sign that something is wrong is that our calls are not returned and our texts not responded to. This is what Malcolm Sentance would experience as that gloomy March day wore on, with his calls to Jane unanswered and the voicemail messages that he had left on her mobile phone ignored.

When Malcolm returned home at 3.40 that afternoon, there was no sign of Jane but he was not too worried. But as afternoon became evening his concern led him again to the phone. After fruitlessly calling friends and family, none of whom had heard from or seen Jane, he sat back in his armchair, by now deeply troubled. It was completely unlike Jane to have her phone switched off; even at the school where she taught, she would keep the mobile's silent facility in operation – especially for him.

Contact by phone during the day was a precious thing to them both. Now Malcolm just could not dispel the feeling that all was not well, that Jane was in some kind of trouble.

When the clock struck midnight and there was still no sign of, or message from, Jane, he picked up the phone once again, this time to call the police. Though they were sympathetic, Jane's disappearance was initially treated as a routine missing-person inquiry. But, as the weekend passed, with Malcolm in a state of near-panic, a disturbing realisation began to dawn on him.

Five full days after Jane Longhurst vanished, a major police investigation was launched. Officers occupied eight rooms at the Sussex Police Headquarters, and 20 detectives were initially assigned to what had been labelled Operation Keen. Since Jane's disappearance, it was ascertained that her bank account had not been touched, her mobile phone was switched off and it did not appear that she had taken any of her personal property, which would have suggested she was leaving Malcolm.

The police had pondered over every possible reason why Jane might simply vanish as she had. The two obvious possibilities were that she had been abducted and killed or that she had willingly accompanied someone and then been murdered. It seemed more likely that she had gone with someone of her own accord because, police later surmised, her physical fitness and strength would have ensured she would not have been taken off without a struggle.

Of course, a blow to the head or a threat from a weapon could equally have ensured her subjugation, but there was no indication that either had occurred. Therefore it seemed prudent to assume that someone had manipulated Jane Longhurst into a position where she could be physically controlled.

As time went on and the circumstances surrounding Jane's disappearance became more suspicious and the chances of her being dead increased, the missing-person inquiry became a murder investigation and about 20 more detectives were assigned to what was now dubbed Operation Mystic. Up to 70 officers were now involved in the search.

Police helicopters clattered over areas throughout the county and fingertip searches were undertaken in parks, railway cuttings, woods and forests, but very few clues were unearthed.

In order to assist the inquiry, the *Argus* newspaper in Brighton agreed to distribute hundreds of wanted posters featuring the missing woman.

After four weeks in which nothing tangible had emerged, Sussex Police pledged £5,000 for information as they made a renewed appeal for help in finding Jane.

The following Thursday, Detective Inspector Chris Standard, who was heading the investigation, said at the first of a number of televised press conferences, 'We hope that, by putting up this reward, we will prompt someone's memory and subsequently locate Jane – that is the main focus of our inquiry.'

Malcolm, and Jane's mother and sister, joined a news conference to appeal for help. When this achieved virtually nothing, to say the police were surprised would be an understatement. DI Standard admitted that in his 25-year-career as a police officer he had never known anything like it. Normally, appeals such as this produced a wealth of helpful leads. Here there was nothing. It began to seem as though the mystery of what had happened to Jane Longhurst would persist indefinitely.

The officer also admitted that there was by now only a slim chance that Jane was still alive. When he talked about 'finding Jane', he was speaking about finding her body.

Finally, on Saturday, 19 April 2003, everybody's worst fears were confirmed. Jane was found and the circumstances were horrific. She had been discarded like an old mattress in a nature reserve 18 miles from her Brighton home. It seemed impossibly perverse that Jane's lifeless corpse should end up in an RSPB bird sanctuary.

She had been throttled to death and her charred, still smouldering corpse had very recently been set alight with the help of a fire accelerant. Firefighters had been called to Wiggonholt Common, near Pulborough, West Sussex, at 8.30pm after a motorist spotted a plume of smoke between some trees just off the main road.

At first, the firefighters thought they were dealing with a

mound of rubbish that had been ignited. When it became clear that the blackened remains were those of a human being, they were initially unable to confirm if the body was that of a man or a woman, but the police later confirmed that it was indeed a female.

Jane had been missing for just over five weeks.

As she had been completely stripped of her belongings, police made it clear that they wanted to hear from anyone who may have had knowledge of where her blue Nokia 3310 mobile phone, black Next wallet, shoes and blue denim jacket were.

The following Monday, as tributes were paid to the popular teacher, the officer now leading the inquiry, Detective Chief Inspector Steve Dennis, announced, 'Our job now is to find Jane's killer.' He explained at the press conference that the killer had attempted to dispose of the body as quickly as possible, just before dark. Was the killer afraid of the dark? Of what might be in it for him?

DCI Dennis went on to reveal: 'Jane's been kept somewhere, she's been dead for a long time and she probably died shortly after she disappeared. They have tried to get rid of her in a fit of panic, something spooked them to deposit her where they did, and then they've tried to burn the evidence.'

Ominously, he added that the body had been 'well preserved' for the four or five weeks since the murder.

What had Jane's murderer been doing with her?

DCI Dennis rounded off the conference with a message that police were keen to trace three cars seen in the area where the body was discovered.

A statement from Jane's family, read out at the press conference, said, 'While we expected the worst, none of us could be prepared for how devastating this is. We've lost a devoted daughter, sister and partner. All who knew her loved Jane and she enjoyed life to the full. She will be missed terribly and her death has left a hole in our lives.'

Colleagues of the murdered school teacher paid tribute to her, describing her as a 'delightful, genuine and caring person'.

Still hindered at this point by the lack of a viable suspect in Jane's murder, the police started appealing again. 'Now is the time for anyone with any information about Jane to come forward,' said DCI Dennis. 'As a matter of routine we have been speaking to people who are significant in Jane's life. At this time, however, there are no suspects.'

This is a procedure that occurs in most murder cases. Everybody needs to be eliminated from the inquiry. As police were quick to suggest, it was likely that Jane knew her killer, though they could not rule out the possibility of a stranger being responsible.

In another statement read at a press conference, Jane's mother and her sister, along with Malcolm Sentance, appealed for the person, or persons, who may be harbouring the killer to give him up: 'We are slowly coming to terms with what has happened to Jane and pulling together as a family to support each other during such a difficult time. Our main aim now is to find the person who did this and to make sure justice is done. Recent publicity has prompted a lot of people to come forward and we would reiterate the appeals that the police have been making. Anyone who knows anything about what happened, we beg you to come forward. If you are protecting a loved one, or you think someone is hiding something, try to imagine how you would feel if this was your daughter or partner or sister who has been killed this way. You too would want to find the person who did it. If you know or suspect anything please contact the police.'

When Jane's horribly burned remains were removed from the desolate woodland where they had been dumped, the police undertook a meticulous search of the area. They found some items that were deemed to be part of a 'significant breakthrough'. Among them were the match used to set light to Jane's dead body, a box of matches – presumably where the match had come from – and Jane's wristwatch. The items were rapidly sent for forensic testing. With these finds entered into evidence, DCI Dennis soon made it apparent that his team were 'one step behind' the killer.

'[The items] were found around the area where Jane was set on fire – it may be that they have nothing to do with the inquiry but they could also provide vital clues as to who her killer is,' he said, then, looking pointedly into the television cameras before him, he made a direct appeal to the murderer. 'If you are Jane's killer then please come forward now and speak to us. We want to hear from you and find out what has happened. This is the chance to tell us.'

Following all these impassioned appeals from the police and the victim's family, more than 100 calls were made to Sussex Police in relation to the murder hunt. At first, the information did not seem too encouraging. Then a name came up and the police zeroed in immediately. The name was Graham Coutts. Coutts was the boyfriend of one of Jane's friends, Lisa Stephens, and it was learned that Jane had made a telephone call to the couple's flat on the day she went missing.

It was around this time that another name, Paul Kelly, surfaced, as a result of staff at the Big Yellow Storage Company in Brighton becoming suspicious and alerting the police about an unpleasant smell emanating from the space Mr Kelly had rented. The call was prompted by the extensive coverage surrounding Jane's disappearance.

When officers were dispatched to check the storage unit on Monday, 28 April, they made some crucial discoveries. Mr Kelly had Jane Longhurst's mobile phone there, along with her denim jacket, her purse and her swimming kit. Also found was a bloodstained shirt, later discovered to belong to Graham Coutts. The blood on the shirt turned out to be Jane Longhurst's.

In addition, there was a condom containing semen – Graham Coutts's semen.

A tarpaulin and a roll of adhesive tape were also present in the space, along with a plastic petrol can.

Mr Coutts certainly had some explaining to do, the more so because he had been captured on CCTV purchasing a can of petrol, a toilet roll and bin liners from a Texaco garage next to the King Alfred Leisure Centre in Hove, adjacent to Brighton.

Around 40 minutes after this recording was made, Coutts was seen by a motorist on the common leading to the bird reserve and Jane Longhurst's burning body.

When police initially interviewed 35-year-old Coutts, a former musician, originally from Leven in Scotland, and his girlfriend, Lisa Stephens, it became apparent that they had been friendly with Jane Longhurst and Malcolm Sentance for some five years.

Subsequently, it was learned that it was Coutts who had answered the phone when Jane had called that day in March. On the pretext of joining her for a swim at the local baths, Coutts instead lured Jane to his flat. Unbeknownst to her, he had decided to play some of his favourite games with her and, unfortunately for her, his sexual pleasure was in the front of his twisted mind.

It was in the sanctity of his lair that the pasty-faced deviant with a wolfish smile would enact his lifelong fantasy of strangling a woman to death for sexual pleasure. Against Coutts's demented onslaught, poor Jane stood no chance. She was dragged into the bedroom, hurled down on to the bed and raped. During this ordeal, she was also strangled with a pair of tights.

The savage indignities wreaked on Jane Longhurst would continue long after her death.

Once the police had focused on Coutts as their prime suspect, it was only a short time before he was arrested. He professed to be in shock at the charges levelled at him. From the outset, he denied everything and proved to be a very stubborn interviewee. He was released but shortly afterwards rearrested, and this time the police came down a lot harder on him. They had spoken to a couple of his ex-girlfriends, who had had some very disquieting things to say about the man. He liked to tie them up and partly strangle them, for example. Some smothering during sex with Coutts was not unheard of either.

When police obtained authorisation to search the suspect's home, they discovered, along with more DNA evidence linking him to Jane Longhurst, two home computers. Stored on these were thousands of hardcore pornographic images, the vast majority of which depicted women being brutalised: hanging, suffocation, stabbing all being inflicted on bound, or in some way helpless, women, naked and raped. Some of the women appeared to be dead: covered in blood or with cyanotic hues discolouring their faces as a result of strangulation, their eyes staring glassily into the camera.

These sickening images were discovered after a look at Coutts's online history to trace his recent internet travels. Among the disgusting websites he visited, all of which showed extreme brutality and degradation of women, were pages devoted to rape, necrophilia, hanging and asphyxiation. It was also learned that these were among the sites viewed by Coutts the day before Jane went missing.

Given his obvious interest in violent atrocities committed against young women, the police confronted Coutts with what they had gleaned from his PC. Armed also with the physical evidence they had gathered, they tried to persuade him to at least admit some culpability for Jane's death.

Under questioning, Coutts alternated between reeling off phrases such as 'I really don't want to talk about this with you' and openly weeping. Mostly, though, the part-time salesman with the eerie stare and receding hairline just sat in silence, failing to answer any questions at all.

In the end, he did acknowledge that he had been responsible for Jane's death but insisted that it had come about as a direct result of an accident caused during what he described as 'a mutual fantasy'.

Jane, he said, had consented to being tied up and strangled with a pair of stockings during sex, but he had unfortunately taken it too far. The fact that the tights he used to garrotte the life out of Jane Longhurst had been so deeply embedded in her throat that they had almost disappeared seemed not to dissuade him from trotting out this ludicrous story.

The police knew they were dealing with a sado-sexual homicidal psychopath – one of the most dangerous of all killer breeds. They had recently secured CCTV video footage of

Coutts at the Big Yellow Storage Company in Brighton wheeling around a huge cardboard box. Inside this box was Jane Longhurst, naked, some 11 days after she had been murdered. Coutts, it transpired, had had to remove the decomposing body from his garden shed, where the body had originally been stored, because it had begun to smell.

He later said that he had not wanted to upset his utterly unaware girlfriend, who was expecting twins, with the foul odour of putrefying flesh. Coutts had made the gruesome pilgrimage to the storage facility to abuse the corpse on at least ten occasions. In fact, he only disposed of his victim's body when he feared he might be caught.

His clandestine trips to his garden shed were doubtless spent engaged in similar revolting necrophiliac acts. Despite the horror of what this man had done, he displayed absolutely no remorse in the presence of the police officers who questioned him. They resolved that Coutts, once found guilty, was going to prison for a very long time.

The trial of Graham Coutts began on Monday, 14 January 2004, and emotions were running high in the Crown Court in Lewes, a few miles from Brighton; the sheer fiendishness of the alleged crimes was enough to guarantee the accused a hostile reception.

Flanked by guards, Coutts sat in the dock, quite placid for the most part, dressed in a dark suit and tie. Occasionally, he would put on a pair of black-rimmed glasses which merely served to make him look like a more scholarly version of the sexual deviant the prosecution claimed he was. Though he could easily have passed for a chartered accountant or a respectable businessman, sitting there so smartly attired, no one was fooled – he seemed to exude an air of malevolence as his eyes swam behind the lenses of his spectacles.

The first issue the Crown dismantled was Coutts's categorical denial that he had murdered Jane Longhurst to satisfy a macabre fascination with strangled and dead women. He claimed instead, as he had earlier to the police, that Jane had consented to 'asphyxial' sex during which he tied a pair of tights around her neck. He did admit storing Jane's body in his shed and, later, a box for 35 days after her death, before setting it alight with petrol and a match.

Two of Jane's former boyfriends were called. Lincoln Abbotts told the court that he had had a 'normal' sex life with her. At no point had they incorporated, or even discussed, asphyxia or strangulation in their lovemaking. And a written statement from Michael Downe confirmed the same thing. He and Jane had never spoken of bondage, or anything of that nature.

It was starting to look as though Graham Coutts had made an error of judgement when it came to Jane Longhurst's sexual proclivities. Either that or he had fabricated this whole disparaging assault on Jane's memory in an attempt to conceal his own loathsome perversions.

To highlight Coutts's long-term pattern of depraved behaviours and lend additional credence to the idea of the man's inherent lusts, the prosecution called two of the defendant's former sexual partners to the stand. One of these women, 51-year-old Sandra Gates, ensured that the jury gained a most disturbing insight into the real Graham Coutts.

Mrs Gates drew an indelible portrait of the man she had once been intimate with. Speaking of her years with Coutts, she would reveal how he always liked to go to bed first, lying secretly in the dark, waiting for Sandra to join him. This sense of anticipation, this thrill at being able to frighten, is almost universal in sexual psychopaths.

The American serial killer Ted Bundy, when he wasn't raping and murdering untold numbers of women, would often sneak up on a girlfriend or jump out of bushes to scare her. He also liked to tie her up with stockings and would sometimes choke her during intercourse.

Graham Coutts was no different in his bedroom exploits. 'Put on your white panties and stockings, babe,' he would whisper out of the darkness. Sandra knew what was coming. She had endured this ritual before. As Graham instructed her to kneel on the floor, he slid quietly out of the bed and crept through the dark room towards her.

He would materialise like a phantom behind her, signalling his presence by suddenly stroking her neck – an area of the body he had already alluded to having an intense fetish for. 'I'm gonna put something around your neck now, babe,' he rasped. A pair of tights would then be wound around her throat and Coutts would begin throttling her. 'Keep quiet now, darling,' he would pant, clearly in ecstasy as he slowly constricted his girlfriend's breathing.

For six long years, Sandra remained with Coutts, tolerating his twisted sex games and perverse fantasies, mainly as a means of avoiding his violent rages. It seemed her lover had quite a temper when he didn't get his own way.

Like so many other killers of this ilk, Coutts was described by Sandra as being 'very charming… on the surface'. Underneath the flimsy veneer, however, lay a ruthless pervert who would one day realise his morbid aspirations.

In court, Sandra described herself as being emotionally

vulnerable when she had first met Coutts, 16 years earlier, in The Wick pub in Brighton. He was a young guitarist who played in some of the local bands and he made quite an impression on the lonely, divorced mother of five. Sandra was Graham's senior and was surprised and flattered by his attentions.

'Graham seemed like a nice young man,' she said, her voice shaking ever so slightly. 'He didn't seem remotely strange and we'd chat about music. If anything, he was shy and bashful.' At first she rejected his advances because 'I thought I was far too old for him'.

But Coutts knew what he wanted. He was persistent and Sandra reluctantly agreed to meet him for lunch one day. 'He told me he earned a lot of money as a window salesman and owned his own house. I was very impressed that someone so young was so successful. I enjoyed his company. He was clever, articulate and had a very dry sense of humour – very mature for his age.'

Sandra felt particularly fragile after her husband left her. She'd met him when she was 18 and at that time knew nothing of dating. 'Graham was very flattering and would tell me how attractive I was. I fell for it,' she whispered almost guiltily.

Six weeks after she met Coutts, they had sex for the first time at his home in Peacehaven, a town just outside Brighton. 'It was very normal, missionary-position sex,' Sandra told the court. 'There was no sign that he had this fetish for strangulation during sex. That only started a year later. He was very careful to introduce it gradually. But his sex drive was just unbelievable. He wanted sex every day and would even masturbate in front of me. I stupidly thought all young guys were like that.'

Three months into their relationship, Coutts moved in with Sandra.

'At first we were quite happy. Graham could be great when he joined in [with our] family life…' she said, adding, after some thought, 'Though there was evidence of a brooding, anti-social side to him.'

She remembered, 'Other times he was very controlling, refusing to share things and yelling at the kids.' But it seemed that her lover's good side outweighed the bad and, besides, Sandra was scared of being alone again.

Over time, however, she became very disturbed by her partner's strange sexual kinks. She noted, for example, that he would become aroused whenever she was upset. 'I was crying one night and he was cuddling me, when suddenly he announced he had an erection. That set a pattern. He would upset me to turn himself on. He also became very controlling with me and the children, telling us not to have a shower or a bath, to save money. Over time he isolated me from friends and family and made me change my appearance. He liked women to wear thick, black tights, short skirts and have short, spiky hair. The sex also got more bizarre as time went on. At first he would stroke my neck during sex, then move on to putting his hands around my neck. He used to like the lights off and for me to be silent. I was nervous but it never went as far as me passing out. I never lost consciousness but feared I would. I'm lucky he didn't kill me. He told me asphyxiation would improve my orgasms but it did nothing for me. It seemed to please him and the longer we were together the more intimidated I became.'

Focusing hard on these difficult memories, Sandra bravely continued, telling of how Coutts would stare blankly into space during these episodes, obviously very far away in his imaginary world. If ever she requested him to stop, he would reluctantly accede to her wishes, but only after maintaining his grip on her throat for a while longer.

Coutts, it was noted, also derived pleasure from tightening stockings and white cotton knickers around Sandra's neck and, as always, he relished any opportunity to frighten her. This was something at which he had become quite skilled.

On one occasion, he shoved a pillow over her face during sex. Sandra panicked, struggling hard. Coutts finally relented, but that odd gaze of his remained fixed on her.

Now, struggling to retain her composure and taking occasional sips of water from the cup provided by the court usher, Sandra went on, 'I suppose I tried to keep him happy so he wouldn't be shouting at the kids all the time. If I refused to let him have sex, he would only persist until he got his way.'

Like so many other women who have had relationships with such predators, Sandra questioned her own motives for remaining with this man. 'Why I stayed with him I'll never know. I was frightened. By the end I couldn't sleep and suffered panic attacks.'

Among Coutts's wide-ranging sexual deviations, he was also an accomplished peeping Tom. When asked by the prosecution about his voyeuristic pursuits in the home the coupled shared, Sandra became distraught. 'He used to peep at my girls when they were getting undressed,' she explained. 'He even drilled a hole in the bathroom ceiling to watch them bathing. And he once hid in the wardrobe so he could peek at one of my girls.'

When Sandra became pregnant with Coutts's child, the father-to-be was anything but overjoyed. In fact, he informed her that he did not want children and was emigrating to South Africa. 'As I already had five kids, I had a termination. He came back from South Africa five weeks later and didn't even mention the baby.'

Recounting Coutts's movements around this time, Sandra said that he would disappear often, sometimes for an entire weekend. 'He said he needed space and would go up north, saying he was seeing friends, playing at a gig or visiting his parents in Scotland.'

Coutts could be very secretive about his sojourns 'up north' and would often become quite aggressive if Sandra scrutinised him too closely. Sometimes she would pick up the phone and it would be a girl wanting to speak to Graham. He would explain these calls away, offering that they were 'groupies' who were obsessed by him because he was a musician.

His temper was a force to be reckoned with too. When enraged he would grow very pale and literally froth at the mouth. He would scream obscenities at Sandra, branding her worthless and unstable. The fact that he was the sole cause of her anxieties seemed to go unnoticed by him.

Coutts physically attacked Sandra on a number of occasions. Although she was inevitably distressed by these incidents, nothing he did could compare with the 'emotional battering' that he constantly subjected her to. As an aside to all this terrible abuse, he told Sandra he thought it would be a good idea to get married and, as she later made clear, he was an obsessive list-maker, even going as far as to keep a record of potential wedding guests. 'I would never have married him,' Sandra said firmly. 'Deep down I knew he was mad.'

In 1995, while Coutts was away on business, Sandra made an unpleasant discovery. He had, for some time, kept a locked briefcase under their bed. With him out of the house for a while,

Sandra, whose curiosity had long since got the better of her, took the opportunity to prise open the mystery case. What she found unnerved her.

Inside was a large cache of pornographic snapshots of girls 'trussed up'. On one photograph Coutts had taken the liberty of drawing a ligature around the neck of a girl he worked with.

This doodling and doctoring of photographic images is fairly common among perverted sexual fantasists. Gerard Schaefer, a former Florida sheriff's deputy and serial murderer whose grisly signature was to hang the girls he murdered, was shown to have kept a collection very similar to Coutts's. Schaefer had even drawn crude nooses around the necks of models in magazines to accommodate his burgeoning preoccupation with the asphyxiation of young women.

Then there was one of Coutts's meticulous lists with each of the girls' names on it, all in sequence. When Sandra confronted him about this sinister trove, he reacted with typical melodrama, begging her for forgiveness and insisting that he could never harm anyone, that the pictures were just fuel for fantasies he kept safely stored in his brain. There was no danger of them ever spilling over into reality and engulfing somebody. Honestly, it was the truth. He even promised to seek help, he told her.

A few nights later, however, with the storm apparently over, Coutts wandered into the bedroom with that familiar strange look in his eye. When Sandra asked him what was wrong, she was met with a vicious punch to the eye that sent her reeling. As she lay there on the carpet, shocked and hurt, Coutts let her know that he had a strong feeling he was going to rape and kill someone before long. He then abruptly turned and left the bewildered woman where she lay.

Later, after a phone call from his father and with the deranged Coutts crying and mumbling incoherently, it was decided once and for all that he needed psychological help. Coutts, in fact, went as far as actually making an appointment but later refused to attend when he learned that the psychologist was a woman.

In the end, his doctor prescribed a course of antidepressants. But he would not take them, telling Sandra that he was worried they might negatively affect his sex drive. Despairing, Sandra finally ended her relationship with this human pressure cooker in April 1996, when her 18-year-old son Daniel died.

Daniel had absolutely despised Coutts and the intolerable atmosphere he brought to the home. The teenager spent long periods away from the house in order to escape this egotistical interloper and ultimately drifted towards crime as an outlet. Tragically, he was to fall to his death from a rooftop during a burglary. 'I often wonder if Daniel would have turned to crime if Coutts hadn't been living with us,' Sandra later said. 'He really hated him.'

Soon after Daniel's death, and probably sensing that Coutts felt it was about time to move on to victimise someone else, Sandra ordered her partner to leave her home. Coutts readily agreed.

When he met Lisa Stephens, his love of dangerous sex games did not, of course, diminish, and through her he met Jane Longhurst. Jane fitted his fantasy-female profile to a T. From the moment he saw her, it was quite simply a case of biding his time. As the urges within this fledgling homicidal madman grew, the visage of lovely Jane Longhurst burned within him. One day he would have her. When he was finally ready to explode, her name was at the very top of his list.

After Sandra Gates's testimony, one of the items on the agenda at Court 1 was the reassembling of the jury at the Big Yellow Storage Company in Brighton. The prosecution wanted them to witness the conditions under which Jane's desecrated corpse had been stashed.

Judge Richard Brown had agreed to this request for the jury to visit the premises where Jane had been left in a large cardboard box sealed with heavy-duty tape. However, the storage unit had since been rendered unusable, so they viewed the premises of a similar unit belonging to the company. Accompanied by counsel for the defence and the prosecution, they examined the kind of conditions that Coutts, under his false name of Paul Kelly, had returned to time and time again, utilising an 'out-of-hours' key to enter the unit and commit further atrocities on Jane's decomposing body.

During the 13-day trial, the jury were also given a graphic demonstration by forensic scientist Roger Ide of how a pair of tights found with Jane's corpse had been tied around her neck. To simulate this chilling act he used a plastic drinks bottle wrapped in foam and filled with water; this was to represent a human neck. He then proceeded to knot a pair of tights around the bottle.

Addressing the court, Ide suggested that Jane must have been either upright and face-to-face with her killer as he applied the ligature, or lying on her back, after concluding that a half-knot had been tied in the tights to the front side of her neck.

This image of Coutts kneeling over Jane as he strangled the life from her was a very potent one indeed. Mr Gold, for the defence, attempted to conjure a degree of co-operation between the two parties but Ide disagreed. 'No!' he said firmly. 'The victim was intimidated, overpowered, or forced.'

A pathologist later told the court how she had to use scissors to cut the cruelly knotted implement of death from Jane's neck.

Given that there was overwhelming physical evidence coupled with the numerous CCTV images of Graham Coutts's various murder-related outings, the case really looked like it could only go one way; and a startling image captured by cameras at Big Yellow showed Coutts hefting along his trophy box. The fact that Jane Longhurst was inside it must have seared the gravity of what was being viewed into every member of the jury.

It was time next to turn to the defendant's hoard of gruesome internet porn. The prosecution suggested an 'obvious parallel between the images Coutts chose to access on his computer and the scene that confronted him at the storage location.' Briefly eyeing Coutts, who sat with his head down, the prosecution turned back to the jury and added, 'He acted out, for real, on the unfortunate Jane Longhurst, the fantasies on his computer, the strangling, the killing and the raping of her.'

Under cross-examination, Coutts maintained the fiction that all this stemmed from a mutually agreed sex game that had gone tragically wrong, and at one point he even managed to summon tears as he spoke of Jane.

The jury were unmoved.

On Wednesday, 4 February 2004, they returned a unanimous verdict: guilty of murder. Coutts displayed no visible emotion as Judge Brown quickly passed a mandatory life sentence with a recommended minimum of 30 years to serve.

And he had some final words for Graham Coutts: 'By persisting in your denial and making her [Jane's] loved ones relive her last moments, and the unbelievable degradation of her body, you have shown not a jot of remorse… everything that this court has heard about Jane Longhurst shows her to have been the sort of person whose life enriched all those who came into contact with her. Her undoubted love of her partner, her music and her life screamed out of every page of evidence I have heard on this case.'

Focusing sternly on the man in the dock, he continued, 'In seeking perverted sexual gratification by way of your sordid and evil fantasies, you have taken her life and devastated the lives of those she loved and of those who loved her.'

As Coutts was escorted from the witness box, he was jeered and shouted at by members of the gallery. There were yells for him to face Jane's stricken family and he was called a 'pig' and a 'pervert' by Sandra Gates as he was led away to begin his new life behind bars.

After the trial, Jane's boyfriend, Malcolm Sentance, said he had had a very difficult time in court watching as all the evidence was presented and having to 'swallow his tongue' where Coutts, whom he described as 'subhuman', was concerned. In reference to the killer's outrageous assertion that Jane had willingly submitted to his desires, Sentance said, 'That's the biggest insult. Coutts is a devious man. There's no truth in anything he said from the word go. If it wasn't for the internet, Jane would still be alive. But until 50 women are rounded up, raped and murdered I don't suppose anyone will act. I hope Coutts doesn't kill himself. I want him to suffer for 30 years.'

Jane's mother, Liz Longhurst, said Coutts was 'vile and disgusting'. Seventy-two-year-old Mrs Longhurst, who had sat in court throughout the trial, described her daughter as a beautiful person who was loved by everybody who knew her. She said, 'Today is a relief for us all. We have had one of the most difficult years that we have had to endure.' As Mrs Longhurst continued fighting back her tears, she said, 'I feel pressure should be brought to bear on internet service providers to close down or filter out these pornographic sites, so that people like Jane's killer may no longer feed their sick imaginations.' She added, 'They [internet service providers] must take some responsibility. Hopefully, we can now campaign to end this despicable use of the soul.'

Sandra Gates, who had endured the monster for far too long, commented, 'I was shocked but not surprised that he finally killed someone.'

Indeed, considering how deeply entrenched his fantasies were, it is extremely likely that, if undetected, Coutts would have gone on to kill again and again to satisfy his terrible lust for dead females.

'I tried to make him seek help but he wouldn't,' Sandra continued. 'Now a lovely girl is dead. Everyone says it could have been me.' She ended by saying, 'He is an evil, perverted psychopath and is where he belongs, in prison. Hopefully, he will never be able to hurt another woman again.'

Detective Chief Inspector Steve Dennis, who had led the case, was in complete agreement, saying that 'a very dangerous man' had been removed from society.

Looking back into Graham Coutts's recent history, it is possible to see a warning of a tragedy to come. Seven years before murdering Jane Longhurst, he had unceremoniously intruded into the life of a lady named Georgina Langridge, and she had never forgotten it.

When Mrs Langridge caught Coutts secretly filming her daughters in a changing cubicle at a public swimming pool, she yelled at him. He had been poking the camera over the top of the cubicle, videoing her daughters as they undressed. Confronted by the irate mother, the Peeping Tom fled but was quickly arrested by police after poolside staff contacted them.

Subsequently, he was charged with the offence but was later acquitted by magistrates. On learning of this, Mrs Langridge was swift in writing to them. Her letter shows remarkable foresight into the misdeeds of a fledgling sexual criminal. In part of her letter, she had angrily written, 'History often proves that this type of behaviour continues, you now have to look to yourselves… and therefore accept responsibility for any further offences this person will commit.'

After the trial, Liz Longhurst would have a meeting with then Home Secretary David Blunkett, who was very keen to stamp out violent online pornography. Following a brief investigation, it was agreed that Blunkett would take his findings to the USA and call for a clampdown on sick internet websites, the view being taken that the two countries are jointly responsible for the spirit of lawlessness. After a meeting with the Deputy Attorney General, Jim Comey, it was agreed that they should take this step.

The Home Office has claimed that websites devoted to necrophilia are rare but did warrant action. (The authors can confirm that there are more of these sites than most people would like to believe.)

The Home Office official spokesman said, 'We have agreed that a specific group of officials would meet jointly to work out what the next stage would be. We agreed that we would put our heads together to get some action on the issue. The Deputy Attorney General said it was something they had been increasingly concerned about. Experts make clear however that this kind of manoeuvre can be difficult legally, especially if sites are hosted overseas.'

The head of the National Hi-Tech Crime Unit recently said that websites devoted to necrophilia and cannibalism are 'corrupting vulnerable people and should be closed'. Chief Superintendent Len Hynds, who heads the unit, says, 'For the internet to continue to grow as a mainstream medium for businesses, education and entertainment, it must design out the minority factors that inhabit cyberspace for their own perverse gratification.'

But, as one IT security manager has commented, 'On the pragmatic side, just how do they think that this can be enforced – it wasn't christened the "worldwide web" without good reason. Like all "vices" they will always find an outlet and a supplier for the depraved and corrupt in society. Let's stop wasting our time and effort on what we can't control and go for the organised crime syndicates that peddle this filth.'

The Internet Watch Foundation also warned that, from a legal position, a complete cessation of these kinds of sites could be very complicated. 'At the IWF we do sometimes receive complaints about websites and material which contains adult content, but unless they are hosted in the UK and may potentially be "borderline extreme" in terms of content, i.e. it is unclear as to whether the images may be illegal, it is not within our remit to further investigate these sites.'

A further statement read, 'Due to the increasing diversity in social attitudes, "adult" content, the context in which it is viewed and possessed and any "influence" it may have, is very difficult to govern.'

While society is now protected from Graham Coutts, the myriad deviant websites he habitually patronised are still fully accessible. It seems that Mr Blunkett and Mr Comey have not had quite the impact on internet-based purveyors of violent pornography that they intended.

There must be scores of latent sex monsters waiting to emerge into the real world once their daily diet of internet horrors is no longer enough to quench their dark and morally perverse cravings. The beast that is Graham Coutts was just one of them.

The tragic case of Jane Longhurst raises more questions than it provides answers. Clearly, Jane was a thoroughly decent and lovely young woman whose precious life was brought to an end at the hands of a depraved monster. This loss can never be replaced. However, I am obliged to focus this postscript more towards the worthless Graham Coutts than his victim, for we can learn much from his behaviour.

Clearly, Coutts was a man predisposed towards anti-social behaviour, as this account has shown, whose tendencies were catered for by certain websites. It is also correct to say that many individuals of his ilk commit similar crimes without being exposed to pornography published on the internet. We only have to look at other men – Ted Bundy, Michael Bruce Ross, Ed Kemper and legions of others who have been exposed to pornography through magazines and video – to know that before the advent of the internet the same types of sex-related murders were being committed.

Invariably, most of these offenders shift the blame for their actions on to their exposure to pornography, as Ted Bundy has stated unequivocally, 'I was exposed to pornography for years. It led me to my violent ways.'

The argument as to whether long periods of exposure to hardcore porn encourages or triggers rape or sexual homicide has led to a division of opinion into two main camps. There are those who say that there is no empirical evidence to support the contention that exposure to this type of material encourages and triggers these crimes. The other side maintains the opposite.

I would be failing in my role as a criminologist if I did not highlight the obvious fact that millions of men, and a smaller number of women, do enjoy access to hardcore pornography, whether through the internet or through other media, and this appears to have no adverse effects on them as far as anti-social behaviour is concerned.

This being said, we are quite sure most will agree that for a minority of people – those with a latent disposition to committing such offences, as well as those without the normal psychological balancing mechanisms enjoyed by most of us, coupled with low self-esteem and, perhaps, underlying psychiatric problems – exposure to hardcore porn of the kind enjoyed by Graham Coutts is extremely destructive indeed.

Going further, Steven Morris, my co-author, has made an interesting and, I believe, valid observation. He suggests that people like Coutts who harbour such destructive fantasies may actually find support for their warped thinking when visiting these sites which boast tens of thousands of seemingly like-minded users.

'Subconsciously, Coutts felt he was joining some kind of club,' says Steven. 'With his already predisposed warped mindset, these sites started to legitimise his way of thinking.'

This is a perceptive line of thought, and the same rationale may be applied to other types of website, for those concerned with giving help to would-be suicides and with euthanasia offer similar 'membership-type' content that implies 'that one is not alone'. For loners, in most cases people who are lacking in connection with the real world, these sites become very powerful influences and motivators.

For most people, visiting these sites is merely a 'healthy' outlet for their fantasies and no real long-term harm is done. However, there will always be a few individuals – as is illustrated by the cases of the cannibal Armin Meiwes and his victim; the suicidal Suzy Gonzales; and Sharon Lopatka, who wanted to be murdered by an internet lover – who will go beyond the norm, however extreme the 'norm' on the internet might appear to be.

Whether Coutts would have killed Jane had he not visited the sites he did is a matter for conjecture – we cannot get inside his head and read his mind. But we can say with confidence that his exposure to these sites pushed him further into his fantasy world.

And it is here that I would like to leave you with a few chilling facts. Please make of them what you will.

There are over 80,000 websites dedicated to snuff rape and killings, cannibalism and necrophilia.

Law-enforcement agencies in the USA, including the FBI, the Customs Service and the National Criminal Intelligence Service (NCIS), say that medium- to long-term exposure to pornography can trigger sex crimes, including serial rape and sexual homicide.

It is interesting to note that the FBI found that 81 per cent of the serial murderers they interviewed had been exposed to pornography for long periods and indulged in compulsive masturbation.

Every single day of the week, thousands more men, and some women, are committing sex-related crimes, including rape and murder, after exposing themselves to internet pornography, when, without the exposure, they would not have done so.

X-rated internet pornography is a cancer. But there seems to be no way to cut out this social disease and the number of crimes involved is growing exponentially: at any one time over three thousand such crimes are listed on internet pages. Almost every US state has sites dedicated to listing internet-generated sex crimes within its legal jurisdiction. (Of course, this is just the tip of the iceberg, for there is also a thriving world of sexual offences not related to the internet.)

In 2003, the web filtering service N2H2 reported that the number of pornographic web pages topped 260 million and that the figure was still growing at an unprecedented rate. N2H2's database contained 14 million identified pages of pornography in 1998, so the growth to 260 million represents an almost 21-fold increase in just five years. In five years' time… well, you can work that out for yourself.

For an individual interested – and many are well and truly hooked – in all forms of pornography, this is the equivalent of having instant access to pornographic books and magazines offering a total of 260 million pages of illicit material and images – with hundreds more such publications, covering every conceivable sexual subject, being delivered daily to his home.

Long gone are the days when Dad popped down to the newsagent to collect his fishing magazine and returned home to discreetly slip a copy of *Playboy* under the bedroom carpet.

At the time of writing there are more than 1.3 million porn

websites, and N2H2 says that more than 32 million individuals visited at least one in September 2003 – figures for 2005 are not yet available – and of these nearly 22.8 million (71 per cent) were male.

SUZY GONZALES: INTERNET SUICIDE

'I'm no toothpick supermodel, though. I am just your average Joan who has everything to lose and is willing to lose it for absolutely no reason. I am tired. I want to sleep.'

Suzy Gonzales in a suicide note

It was bound to happen. First, proponents of the culture of death brought us physician-assisted suicide (PAS). Now we must contend with IAS – internet-assisted suicide. For the promotion and facilitation of self-destruction has entered cyberspace. And how indifferent to the value of human life certain segments of our society have grown, and how callous they are when faced with a despairing person driven to contemplate suicide.

First they bestow moral permission.

Then they teach the intending suicide how to do it.

Finally they keep the person company until the deed is done.

It is the modern version of the howling crowd yelling 'Jump! Jump!' at the suicidal figure standing on the window ledge of a tall building.

Wearing a fuchsia wig and carrying a stuffed two-headed cat that she'd stitched together from scratch, 19-year-old Suzy Gonzales zipped around the small ranching town of Red Bluff, Florida, on a red scooter. She came from a tight-knit family, favoured tartan skirts with green sneakers, had earned a full scholarship to Florida State University and possessed a radiant smile.

But she was severely depressed and wanted to kill herself.

Unbeknownst to her loved ones and friends, the teenager logged on to an obscure internet site to confide her darkest thoughts to strangers. There she found people who told her that suicide was an acceptable way to end her despair, and who gave her instructions on how to obtain a lethal dose of potassium cyanide and mix it into a deadly cocktail.

If this sounds vaguely familiar, it should. America's assisted-suicide advocacy groups have promoted the idea of suicide as the 'ultimate civil right' for years. And, just as the denizens of the internet site taught Suzy Gonzales how to kill herself, some publications have long instructed readers how to commit suicide, while conventions regularly feature guest speakers who bring their newly invented suicide machines for conventioneers to ooh and aah over. The devices are a much favoured, and almost instantly available, method of self-dispatch.

During the early hours of Sunday, 23 March 2003, after she cleaned her apartment and fed her kittens, Gonzales checked into a Tallahassee motel, where she stirred the poison into a glass of tap water, checked its acidity with a pH meter and drank it.

Her family, her best friend and the Tallahassee Police were notified of her death by time-delayed emails that she had prepared with the help of another member of the online community.

'One last note – I will make this short, as I know it will be hard to deal with. If you haven't heard by now, I have passed away.

'I know I should have told you, but I have been depressed and suicidal for a long, long time – it is all right to be sad and it is all right to cry. These types of things tend to happen, and it really isn't that big of a deal. Death is just another part of life.'

Gonzales's is the fourteenth confirmed suicide associated with the online discussion group, which the authors do not identify. An additional 14 suicides are listed as 'success stories' but cannot be verified because the individuals used anonymous screen names and the group has refused to disclose their identities.

In fact, the number of suicides linked to the group may be higher. There is evidence that at least one person, who never actually communicated with the group, killed herself after downloading its instructions on how to commit suicide by inhaling carbon monoxide.

Founded in 1990, the group defines its philosophy as being 'pro-choice' as regards suicide. Participants view the act as a civil right that anyone should be able to exercise, for whatever reason.

Every day the internet site is filled with hopeless rants about life's miseries, advertisements for suicide partners and requests for feedback on self-murder plans. Among the hottest items is a 'Murder Methods file', a step-by-step guide on how to commit suicide, by methods ranging from asphyxiation to rat poison.

The group vigorously defends itself, citing what it sees as a need for people to express suicidal thoughts without fear of being hospitalised by their therapists or alarming their families. But mental-health experts, and the relatives of group members who have died, charge that the group actually encourages depressed people to kill themselves.

The suicide group that Suzy Gonzales found has made a few headlines outside America. In one case, a 20-year-old Norwegian man placed an ad for a suicide partner. It was answered by a 17-year-old Austrian girl, the two met and in February 2000 they flung themselves off Norway's 1,900-foot Pulpit Rock.

A year later a German man and a Californian woman, both in their forties, made a similar pact and shot themselves dead in a Monterey hotel.

Again in America, a 30-year-old unemployed salesman drove to a campsite overlooking the scenic Colorado River, lit the two charcoal grills he had stowed in his car and closed the windows. He died from inhaling the noxious gases.

Then there was the English teenager who hanged himself. Just before doing so, the 17-year-old created a website that opened with the message: 'Hi, and welcome to the homepage of my death.'

Suzy Gonzales first contacted the group on 12 January 2002, when she started a survey entitled 'Why Do You Want To Die?' She answered her own question first.

'I'm bored. I am bored with life,' she wrote. 'I cannot possibly think of anything I want to do that is worth doing. I just want to sleep all day.' She added that she was tired, sad and could enjoy nothing.

Over the next two months, Suzy sent more than 100 messages to the group. She described taking antidepressants that didn't improve her mood, dropping out of Florida State University, where she was studying maths and meteorology, and calling a suicide hotline about 'a friend' before losing her nerve and hanging up to cry.

'I have a wonderful family who will support me in all that I do,' she wrote. 'I make enough money to get by. I have a few close, excellent friends. I'm not hideous nor morbidly obese. I'm no toothpick supermodel, though. I am just your average Joan who has everything to lose and is willing to lose it for absolutely no reason. I am tired. I want to sleep.'

Like the relatives of other members of the online group who have killed themselves, Mike and Mary Gonzales had no idea of their daughter's involvement with it until after her death.

When Suzy's father, a robust 43-year-old retired firefighter, speaks of the online group, rage simmers beneath his controlled exterior. 'She went to that group, and it was like throwing gasoline on a fire,' said Mike Gonzales, whose own father died from a long-term illness a week before his daughter killed herself. 'I'm all for free speech, but, once you start telling young impressionable kids how to kill themselves, that's crossing the line. Someone should be held accountable.'

Mike Gonzales was particularly close to his daughter. They frequently chatted online and by telephone. Such was his devotion to Suzy that, when she became distressed after the September 11th terrorist attacks, he flew across the country and drove her back home to be with her family.

Mary Gonzales, a 50-year-old hospital administrator, believes that, if her youngest girl could have held on a little longer, she would have learned to navigate the ebbs and flows of life and blossomed into a strong, soulful woman. Instead, she stumbled across an online group that told her that life was not worth living.

'They [the group] never told her that people do work through depression and get better and go on to live happy lives,' said Mary, whose voice often dissolves into silence when she tries to put into words what happened. 'They never gave her hope.'

It took several attempts, Suzy wrote to the group, but she was able to order potassium cyanide online as well as a pH meter, 'so I can be sure that the concoction isn't too basic/acidic for my throat'.

To get the materials, Gonzales used a trick recommended by other group members.

Posing as a jeweller, she ordered the cyanide online, ostensibly to polish metal. She also requested several other chemicals to make her order look genuine. Her order, billed to Winston Jewellers, didn't raise a red flag at the Massachusetts chemical manufacturer that sold her the poison.

'All the materials she ordered points to a legitimate jewellery operation,' said Darrell Sanders, who oversees chemical sales at Alfa Aesar. 'She fooled me – and it hurts, emotionally.'

Suzy patterned her suicide after another member of the group, Dave Conibear, who killed himself in 1992. The 28-year-old Canadian software engineer detailed online the exact proportions of his cyanide concoction. He timed a message to be delivered to the group after his death, and even programmed his computer to dial 911, the emergency services' number.

Two weeks before she died, Suzy cryptically signed her message '2 weeks seven days', before she signed off with 'one week'.

On 21 March she wrote, 'Today, I feel great. Besides feeling a bit light-headed, I feel good. The sun is shining, the air is warm. It feels like such a nice day to just lie in the sun. To quote Richie

Tenenbaum, "I am going to kill myself tomorrow." I've stopped taking my meds so I'm not happy and decide that life is not worth living. I will just get down again someday… I am preventing that.'

Suzy Gonzales last talked to her parents on the evening of 22 March, explaining that she was looking for air tickets to return to California for her grandfather's funeral.

The last thing she said to her father was: 'I love you, Dad. I'll see you soon.'

In December 2002, a Kansas woman named Joanne Hossack filed a wrongful-death suit against a member who posted a message to the same group that Suzy had contacted. In the message, the group member said that she had talked on the phone with Hossack's 17-year-old son and 'kept him company' as he intentionally overdosed on drugs. Hossack dropped the case after learning that her son's online friend was also a troubled minor.

In May of that year, two Englishmen, Michael Gooden and Louis Gillies, had met through another group, Alternative Suicide Holidays, and made a pact to jump together off a cliff in East Sussex. But, while 35-year-old Glasgow-born Gooden plunged to his death off Beachy Head in June, 36-year-old Gillies changed his mind at the last minute and narrated the episode in a posting online, saying that 'the act was inspirational'.

Investigators found Gillies's posting and arrested him for violating the UK's Suicide Act, which makes it illegal to aid, abet or counsel another person to commit suicide and carries a jail sentence of up to 14 years.

When Gillies failed to appear in court, police went to his flat in London's West End to find he had hanged himself.

To return to Suzy Gonzales, until 12.01am on 23 March she was conversing online about her deadly itinerary with a member of the suicide group who called himself 'River'. But River did nothing to stop her.

'Suzy had me proofread her notes, and we went over all the details of her exit just to be safe,' he wrote to the group after her suicide, which he referred to as a passage into 'transition'.

The only information that Mike and Mary Gonzales have about River is that he mentioned he was living in central Florida with a wife and an 18-year-old son.

A few minutes past midnight on 23 March, Suzy Gonzales composed her final note to the group. 'Goodnight,' read the subject line.

'Bye everyone, see you on the other side,' she wrote, ending the note with her characteristic '! Suzy'.

'Smooth sailing,' one person online responded.

'I'll be following soon,' replied another sad individual.

Shortly after sending the message, Suzy tucked the can of cyanide into her purse, got into her car and drove to the Red Roof Inn.

In the United States, laws on assisted suicide were passed to prevent people deliberately helping others end their lives by supplying them with a method, such as enough drugs for a fatal overdose, or physically assisting them.

'Simply informing someone how to kill themselves is another matter,' said euthanasia activist Derek Humphrey, who wrote a suicide manual for the terminally ill entitled *Final Exit*.

'I've been monitoring the US assisted-suicide laws for more than 20 years, and it does not appear that counselling is a crime,' he said.

Group members say that discussing their suicidal inclinations online is much easier than in real life.

'When online, I am calm and collected, but give me a couple of seconds of talking about [suicide] in person and it's the same as with the suicide hotline,' Suzy Gonzales wrote ten days before her death. 'I get shaky and start crying. And then I just feel silly – basically, I just need a friend who will understand me.'

These groups 'exist because they wanted to be in a space where they wouldn't be controlled', says Lauren Weinstein, co-founder of People for Internet Responsibility, which studies cyberspace issues. 'Fundamentally, these groups bring with them all the benefits and all the risks that are present with unfettered communication.'

Had Suzy Gonzales told a therapist that she had both a plan and a means to kill herself, she could have been forcibly hospitalised. 'It could be considered malpractice and we could be sued if we didn't,' said Herbert Hendin, medical director for the American Foundation for Suicide Prevention.

Michael Naylor, a psychiatrist at the University of Illinois at Chicago, suggested that Suzy Gonzales's cryptic countdown and repeated recounting of her plans could have been a cry for help that was ignored by the online group.

'The only purpose [this group] serves is helping people to kill themselves,' said Naylor, adding, 'What a lot of these [people] don't seem to realise is that suicide is the last choice you get to make. Once you're dead, you can't undo that. Life isn't a game that can be played over again.'

Suzy sent six time-delayed emails to the Tallahassee Police, telling them that she'd ingested cyanide and that they could find her at the Red Roof Inn. When investigators entered her motel room, they discovered her corpse alongside the poison, which she'd carefully repackaged.

In her email to her parents, Suzy had a request for her memorial service: 'Please play "Fire and Rain"' – James Taylor's elegy to a friend who committed suicide. That friend was named Suzanne, too.

It is a Saturday afternoon in Red Bluff. Banners flutter over the main drag, advertising the high school's presentation of *A Man for All Seasons*. A rodeo is under way at the fairground. And, at a chapel, a sombre crowd gathers to remember Suzanne Michelle Gonzales.

On a table at the front of the room there are dozens of framed pictures – one of Suzy coquettishly pulling up her yellow high-school graduation gown to expose knee-high athletic socks; another where she is a bright-eyed toddler gripping her mother's hand. Near by, the nameless two-headed cat leans against a red scooter. One of the feline's faces is happy – the other not.

Suzy's parents walk into the chapel with a beige urn and place it at the centre of these mementoes of their daughter's life. That same urn had rested between them on the front seat of a U-haul truck as they drove back to California with the contents of Suzy's Florida apartment.

Nancy Hickson, Suzy's high-school speech teacher, recalled for the crowd how Suzy gave her a purple wig after she lost her hair to chemotherapy.

'When I met her, I thought, "Finally, a teen who isn't afraid to be different,"' she recalled. 'Suzy had a creative streak a mile wide.'

John Bohrer, the local Southern Baptist pastor, compared Suzy's quirky humour and zest for life to that of the actress Lucille Ball.

Her best friend, 19-year-old Desiree Sok, described Suzy as a spontaneous fun lover, someone with whom she'd cruise around Tallahassee in the middle of the night blaring ska music and eating doughnuts. Someone who'd swerve on to the shoulder of a dark road and jump out of the car just to chase fireflies.

'I don't think she realised all the memories would stop,' Desiree said, her voice trailing off.

As the slide show of Suzy's life was screened, James Taylor's haunting words and melody provided the soundtrack.

This new and morbid phenomenon of internet-inspired suicide is not confined to the USA. Because of the medium's huge reach it has become a global issue, and yet internet service providers continue to host these sites.

The discovery in 2004 of the bodies of four young men in a car at a viewpoint near Mount Fuji in Japan appeared to be more evidence of a grim new trend in this prosperous country – group suicides of strangers who meet over the internet. The suicide pacts, which have resulted in at least 18 deaths in Japan since February 2004, are shocking to experts, even in a nation already plagued by an astronomical suicide rate.

The victims are normally young and meet over the internet through a growing number of suicide-related sites, chatrooms and bulletin boards in Japanese – sites where participants go online not to dissuade but to support one another in their desire for death.

In the latest confirmed case in early May 2005, the victims were a man of 30 and two women of 22 and 18. None had apparently known the others before meeting online, where they started planning their suicide. As in several other cases, they died of carbon monoxide poisoning from a coal-burning stove after sealing themselves in a room using plastic sheeting and duct tape. Others have taken their lives by the same method – promoted by websites as fast and painless – in cars parked in remote mountain areas.

Some suicide pacts have been averted, or ended in injury but not death, as in the case of two girls, 14 and 17, who jumped together off a five-storey building.

The group WiredSafety, which has 10,000 volunteers around the world visiting online chatrooms watching for people who prey on children, reports that it has come across many Japanese suicide websites, including ones that encourage participants to overdose together in front of webcams.

'We are picking up lot [of suicide sites] that are just in Japanese,' says Parry Aftab, executive director of WiredSafety. 'We report them to local law enforcement, or the ISP to have them take down the sites. But they just pop up someplace else.'

Some websites are expressly for meeting suicide partners, while others suggest the best ways to commit the act, including, for example, where to get the coal stoves and how to prepare the car or other suicide site.

SHARON LOPATKA'S CYBER WORLD

'Hi! My name is Nancy.

'I am 25 have Blonde hair, green eyes am 5'6 and weigh 121. Is anyone out there interested in buying ... my worn ... panties ... or pantihose....??? This is not a joke or a wacky Internet scam. I am very serious about this. If you are serious too you can e-mail me ...!'

MESSAGE POSTED BY SHARON LOPATKA IN AN AREA OF THE INTERNET WHERE SEXUAL EROTICA IS THE MAIN TOPIC

'I don't know how much I pulled the rope... I never wanted to kill her, but she ended up dead.'

BOBBY GLASS ON THE MURDER OF SHARON LOPATKA

There's not much to Lenoir, North Carolina, a town of 14,000 at the foot of the Blue Ridge Mountains. The monument to the Daughters of the Confederacy in the town square watches over another losing battle, this one economic. Downtown slips silently into the embarrassed embrace of loan companies, storefront churches and used-clothing shops. The stagnant centre is skirted by highways, busy chain stores and fast-food outlets. It would not be quite right to say people in Lenoir are surprised at killings in their midst because they get around six murders a year, even if they could not have dreamed up the scenario that follows.

Rural America no longer is, and maybe never was, quite so sheltered as its apple-pie image suggests. 'People think that, because this is a small town, these things don't happen. It's not true. We have people here no different than the big cities,' said Brenda Watson, who owns the Carolina Cafe at 209 Main Street. 'And I wouldn't let my kids walk alone here at night.'

Indeed, former district attorney Flaherty claims, 'Most of the murders are love triangles, but when Lopatka lost her life she also lost her anonymity, and she was none of the things she claimed to be.'

In fact, according to her autopsy report she was dark-haired with dark eyes set into a heavy face and five foot ten and 189 pounds when she died. And, far from the wild video star she claimed to be, she lived her life quietly in a ranch-style home in Indian Court, a cul-de-sac in the quiet, hilly town of Hampstead, Maryland, where children play tag in front yards, dogs tease the postman and deviancy is a failure to join recycling efforts.

When Lopatka graduated from Pikesville High School in

Baltimore in 1979, her name was Sharon Denburg. She had many friends and was a member of the volleyball and field hockey teams. During her junior and senior years, she was a nurse's aide, a library aide and a singer in the school's chorus.

'She wasn't an outcast or anything of that nature,' said Steven Hyman, who attended school with her. 'She was about as normal as you can get. I think making her this weird loner is just some media thing.'

Sharon Denburg was the oldest of four daughters born to Mr and Mrs Abraham J Denburg in 1961. The family lived in a suburb of Baltimore. Sharon Denburg's parents were devout Orthodox Jews, who were active in the Beth Tfiloh, Baltimore's largest Orthodox Jewish synagogue, where Abraham was a cantor. Sharon had been active in sports, sang in the school choir and was perceived by classmates to be 'as normal as you can get', reported the North Carolina *News & Observer* on 3 November 1996.

In 1991, Sharon wed Victor, a Catholic construction worker from Ellicott City, but her parents did not approve. A former high-school classmate told the *Washington Post* on 3 November 1996 that the marriage was Sharon's 'way of breaking away'. Sharon moved with her husband to a small, ranch-style tract house in Hampstead in the early 1990s. They had no children.

Sharon started up several small internet business ventures from her home to make some extra money. She made a new friend, Diane Safar, who lived near by, and the two of them put together a 30-page booklet on home decorating and country crafts entitled *Dion's Secret of Home Decorating Guide*.

'Here we were decorating our houses one day and talking to each other for advice, and we just said, "Hey, we should put this stuff in a book,"' Safar explained. 'We put it together and then we went around to ladies' groups and churches selling it. It was fun.'

'What I want people to know is the woman I knew was not crazy in the slightest,' Safar said of her friend. 'She was always a happy person, always bubbly even. This person who was killed was not the person I knew.'

In her business called Classified Concepts, Sharon rewrote ad copy for advertisers for $50 per advertisement. She also operated several other websites, where she sold psychic readings and advice. On the sites Sharon would also post ads selling other services, with a premium rate number for which she would receive a percentage of the revenue.

Another way she made money was by advertising pornographic videos.

All varieties of sex were for sale 24 hours a day in Sharon Lopatka's world. She could provide nearly anything anybody desired at any time. With a tapping of her fingers on a computer keyboard, she became five-foot-six and a shapely 121 pounds. A few more taps and she was an aggressive 300-pound dominatrix who promised strict discipline. Or she could tap and become 'Nancy Carlson', a screen actress prepared to star in whatever type of sexual video her fans cared to purchase.

As Nancy Carlson, Sharon sold videos of unconscious women having sexual intercourse. According to the *Augusta Chronicle* of 4 November 1996, one excerpt from an advertisement dated Tuesday, 1 October 1996 stated, 'Hi! My name is Nancy. I just made a VHS video of actual women… willing and unwilling to be… knocked out… drugged… under hypnosis and chloroformed. Never before has a film like this been made that shows the real beauty of the sleeping victim.'

Sharon even went so far as to advertise her own undergarments online, with a message which read, 'Is there anyone out there interested in buying my worn panties?' She certainly had no qualms about advertising and selling products that would appeal to the lurid sexual fetishes of her customers. She also had her own risque sexual fantasies that she actively sought to fulfil:

'DO YOU DARE ENTER... THE LAND OF THE GIANTESS???

'Where men are crushed like bugs... by these angry... yet gorgeous giant goddesses.'

Sharon used the web for a variety of purposes, such as to obtain business ideas and make money. However, she also used it to interact with a larger variety of people who shared her unconventional interests. She often ventured into hardcore pornographic chatrooms where subscribers would openly discuss their interests in necrophilia, bondage, fetishes and sadomasochism.

One of her ads read, 'Let me customise your most exciting TORTURE fantasy for you... on VHS... to watch and enjoy privately in the comfort of your own home. A film designed by you... with scenarios of your choice. Films are shipped in plain envelopes to protect your... privacy.'

She used many pseudonyms and multiple personae in her internet messages. These 'masks' allowed her anonymity and the freedom to pursue her unusual fantasies. According to the *Washington Post* of 3 November 1996, one message Sharon posted stated that she had 'a fascination with torturing till death'.

Over several months, the North Carolina *News & Observer* found more than 50 messages of Sharon's where the overriding theme was that she wanted to be tortured and killed. Often she would post messages looking for a man to satisfy her wish.

'I guess some people have some kind of inner thing going on that you just never know about,' said Debra Walker, Lopatka's neighbour. 'I think we knew them as well as anyone in the neighbourhood. She was just like anyone else you know, and that kind of scares me in a way, to think you really never know somebody.'

A sex-rights activist named Tanith, who often visited the sites, said that she became concerned about Sharon's strange messages. On 3 November 1996, the *Washington Post* quoted Tanith saying that Sharon was 'going to chatrooms and asking to be tortured to death'. Tanith says she had tried to stop her, but Sharon refused. Sharon replied to the woman,: 'I want the real thing. I did not ask for you preaching to me.'

Sharon would sit at her computer typing furiously for hours at a time, trying to make contact with the right person to satisfy her strange desires. Numerous responses to her messages offered to fulfil her fantasy, but the senders withdrew when they discovered that her requests were serious.

Eventually, she found a man who swallowed the bait. Several weeks after meeting him on screen, her last wish was to come true.

She arrived in the foothills of the Blue Ridge Mountains while the foliage was still coloured with brilliant oranges and yellows and reds to meet that man in person. And, police say, in the ultimate fulfilment of her desires, she was bound with rope, made to bleed and then strangled, before her nude body was dumped into a shallow grave.

The internet has been blamed for everything from spreading

recipes for bombs to pushing porn to school kids, but the latest claim, that it contributed to the sex murder of a woman in rural America, sounded like an urban myth. Yet it was all too true.

Early on the morning of Sunday, 13 October 1996, 35-year-old Sharon Lopatka travelled to Baltimore and caught a train to Charlotte, North Carolina, having told her husband that she was going to visit friends in Georgia. A week later, Victor was disturbed to find a mysterious note written by his blonde wife that suggested instead a clandestine, apparently final, trip. 'If my body is never retrieved don't worry,' Sharon had written. 'Know that I am at peace.'

Victor immediately called the police, who looked for evidence as to Sharon's whereabouts on her computer. They found emails suggesting that she had visited someone in Lenoir, North Carolina.

There, on Friday, 25 October 1996, police officers found Sharon's naked, decomposing body buried a short distance from the trailer of the person she had gone to visit. Her hands and feet had been bound with rope and a nylon cord had been strung around her neck. Investigators also found scrape marks around her neck and breasts. The medical examiner determined that she died of strangulation – the violent death Sharon had wished for.

Robert 'Bobby' Frederick Glass was a 45-year-old computer analyst employed by Catawba County, North Carolina. He had worked for the county for almost 16 years and was a productive worker who was responsible for programming tax rolls and keeping track of the fuel consumption of county vehicles.

Bobby was also a computer enthusiast, according to Sherri, his wife of 14 years. But, she lamented, he had more passion for the friend on his desk than for his marriage. Her husband was no longer attracted to her and the final straw, she said, was when her children asked why their father didn't love her any longer.

In May 1996, Bobby and Sherri separated. Shortly afterwards, Sherri left the family home with their three children, daughters aged ten and seven and a son aged six. However, it may have been more than a lack of love that caused the break-up of the family. According to Sherri, there were other marital problems that few had known about; each day Bobby had spent countless hours typing on his computer, and Sherri eventually became suspicious. Bobby subscribed to America Online, a major provider of internet access, and in his net profile he claimed to love photography, music and model railways. In a space reserved for personal quotes he had written, 'Moderation in all things, including moderation.'

One day Sherri logged on and found worrisome emails saved on her husband's hard disk. The messages which had been posted under the pseudonyms 'Toyman' and 'Slowhand' particularly alarmed her because of their 'raw, violent and disturbing' nature.

After dinner one evening, she confronted Bobby. Later, she said that 'all of the colour had drained out of his face'. She realised that there was 'this side to him' that was unknown to her. Despite this alarming discovery, Sherri recalled her husband as 'generally pleasant, hard working and amiable'.

In August 1996, Bobby Glass and Sharon Lopatka became acquainted while visiting sexually orientated internet chatrooms. Bobby displayed a fetish for inflicting pain, whereas Sharon's desire was to be tortured. In an email message to Bobby, Sharon wrote that she wanted to be bound and strangled as she approached orgasm. Bobby responded by describing in detail how he would fulfil her dearest wish.

Correspondence between the two lasted for several months. The police were able to recover almost 900 pages of emails from the warped couple's computers. A senior investigator who worked on the case, Captain Danny Barlow of North Carolina's Caldwell County Sheriff's Department, said, 'If you put all their messages together, you'd have a very large novel with a very sad ending.'

It was discovered that, at about 8.45 on the evening of 13 October, Sharon's train from Baltimore had arrived in Charlotte, where Bobby Glass was waiting, and that they had driven in his pickup truck 80 miles to his trailer home in Lenoir. The events that followed were later to become a source of speculation among police investigators.

On 30 October 1996, the police department's newly developed Computer Crime Unit found substantial evidence in Sharon's computer linking her to Bobby Glass. Police officers monitored Bobby's trailer for several days. It was hoped that Sharon would be found alive there, but she was not seen during the stakeout.

Then Judge Beal issued police with a search warrant for the trailer, and investigators arrived there while Bobby was at work. The ground surrounding the turquoise trailer was littered with rotting garbage and abandoned toys. The interior was equally dirty and cluttered. Among the chaos, police officers found items belonging to Sharon, as well as drug and bondage paraphernalia, child pornography, a pistol and thousands of computer disks.

Seventy-five feet from the trailer, an officer discovered a fresh mound of soil. After digging only 30 inches beneath the mound, they found Sharon's decomposing remains. Caldwell County investigator DA Brown said that, if the body had been buried in the woods behind the trailer, 'we would have never found her'.

That same day Bobby Glass was arrested at his workplace – the first time a police unit had captured a murder suspect primarily on the basis of evidence obtained from emails.

While in custody, Bobby – a member of the Rotary Club, whose sister was a church organist and whose family was well respected throughout the community – was interviewed about the events surrounding the alleged murder of Sharon. He told investigators that for several days he and Sharon had acted out their violent sexual fantasies in his trailer. He confessed that Sharon had willingly allowed him to tie her up with rope and probe her with objects lying around the house. And he revealed that she allowed him to tie a rope around her neck and tighten it as she climaxed during intercourse. But, according to his lawyer, Neil Beach, Bobby claimed to have accidentally strangled Sharon to death, while in the throes of violent sexual play. Later, Bobby was quoted as saying, 'I don't know how much I pulled the rope... I never wanted to kill her, but she ended up dead.'

Sharon Lopatka's body was sent to Dr John Butts, North Carolina's chief medical examiner. The autopsy report stated the cause of death as strangulation. Other tests showed inconclusive evidence of sexual torture or mutilation. Butts believed that Sharon died three days after she arrived in North Carolina.

Attorney Beach said that the autopsy reports supported his client's claim that the death was accidental. 'It is hard for me to believe the woman was tortured for three days if the medical examiner of North Carolina couldn't find any indication of that… It's much easier to understand or picture an accident occurring during sexual activity than it is to conjure up an image of this man as a cold-blooded, premeditated killer,' he said.

Search warrant affidavits released by police stated that Sharon intended to meet Bobby specifically to be tortured and killed. Captain Danny Barlow considered a death under such circumstances to be deliberate, not accidental. According to police, emails written under the pseudonym 'Slowhand' detailing how he was going to kill Sharon provided further evidence that the death was premeditated. Bobby was charged with first-degree murder and held without bond in Caldwell County Jail.

On 26 October, Superior Court Judge Beverly T Beal had issued a gagging order to those directly involved in the case. Despite this, the media obtained enough information to sensationalise the Lopatka case. Most of the news stories focused on the dangers of internet-mediated meetings. Sharon's death spawned debates and discussion groups worldwide. Many called for censorship of the internet to prevent such deaths and to protect children. Conversely, anti-censorship activists argued that the internet was a useful tool, allowing people to express themselves more freely and to voice their ideas in an open forum.

'The Mardi gras phenomenon' is a term used by psychologists to describe the ability to mask oneself and assume a variety of personalities, allowing one to speak and act freely with little or no consequence. This phenomenon is particularly prevalent on the internet, where users can use online chatrooms and news groups to air their opinions and vent their feelings uninhibitedly and in many cases anonymously.

Sharon's death and the publicity surrounding the case led to a growth in interest in understanding deviant sexual behaviours, especially sadism, masochism and the use of asphyxia during sexual intercourse.

The pioneering 19th-century German psychologist Richard von Krafft-Ebing first coined the terms 'sadist' and 'masochist' to describe behaviour in which sexual arousal was achieved through, respectively, the infliction and reception of pain.

According to Reber's *Dictionary of Psychology*, sadism is the association of sexual pleasure with the inflicting of physical and psychic pain on another, including humiliation, exploitation and debasement. Masochism refers to 'any tendency to direct that which is destructive, painful or humiliating against oneself'.

It was Sigmund Freud who was the first to combine the two terms into 'sadomasochism' in order to emphasise the reciprocity of the use of pain during sexual intercourse.

A controversial form of deviant sexual play practised by some sadomasochists employs strangulation. Psychologists use the word 'asphyxiophilia' in connection with sexual strangulation. By this they mean the practice of controlling or restricting oxygen to the brain by 'interfering with the breath directly or through pressure on the carotid arteries' in order to achieve sexual gratification. In many cases, the hands are used or a tourniquet is tied around the throat during intercourse or masturbation to achieve the feeling of euphoria and elation that accompanies a lack of oxygen to the brain. Supposedly, this can increase the intensity of orgasm.

According to *The Deviants' Dictionary*, sexual strangulation practised with a partner is a form of 'edge play', in which one's life is literally in the hands of another. The thrill is said to lie in the danger and vulnerability associated with the activity. However, there have been cases in which edge play has resulted in unintentional death.

The American Psychiatric Association claims that each year in the United States about 250 deaths occur involving strangulation or chokeholds during sexual activity. A large majority of these fatalities have occurred during auto-erotic asphyxiation, in which one restricts one's own oxygen during masturbation, or 'solo play'.

Jay Wiseman, of the Society for Human Sexuality, confirms this finding, saying that only a few of the cases where death occurs as a result of strangulation or a chokehold involve sexual play with a partner.

What makes Sharon Lopatka's case exceptional is that she ventured into the relationship with Bobby Glass with one apparent intention – to die. In short, she was a suicidal masochist. But she was not the first in history to seek out a willing participant who would fulfil a request to be strangled to death for sexual gratification.

Knud R Joergensen wrote in 1995 about the case of composer Franz Kotzwara, who in 1791 enlisted the help of a London prostitute, Susannah Hill, to assist him with his bizarre wish. After paying Hill two shillings, Kotzwara asked her to cut off his genitalia – a request the prostitute refused. Yet Hill did agree to her client's sexual wish to strangle himself with a rope. It was the first documented case of death by sexual strangulation. Hill was eventually arrested for Kotzwara's murder, but later acquitted when the authorities learned that she was more or less an innocent bystander. By contrast, Bobby Glass, 200 years later, faced first-degree murder charges for the sexual strangulation death of Sharon Lopatka, though the charge was eventually reduced to voluntary manslaughter.

The case against Glass included several lengthy delays and dragged on for three years. But on 27 January 2000 he pleaded guilty to voluntary manslaughter, as well as to six counts of second-degree sexual exploitation of a minor that resulted from the discovery of other pornographic material on his computer. He was sentenced to 36 to 53 months in prison for the manslaughter of Sharon Lopatka and 21 to 26 months for the possession of child pornography.

He was sent to Avery-Mitchell Correctional Institution in North Carolina. On 20 February 2002, two weeks before his release, Bobby Glass had a heart attack. He was pronounced dead at 1.30am at Spruce Pine Community Hospital in North Carolina.

Among Sharon's final messages posted on the internet is a note addressed to people who had sent for the videos, failed to receive them and posted their own notes, calling the advertisements a fraud. 'I'm just one person trying to fill all these orders. I don't even have time to HAVE A LIFE,' she complained.

But perhaps the last, poignant word should go to Reverend Clarence Widener, who had officiated at Mr Glass's wedding many years earlier. He said, 'He was a very nice fellow. I don't know what could have happened to him.'

ANASTASIA SOLOVYOVA: IN SEARCH OF A DREAM

'You dragged her to the grave you dug... You stripped her corpse, mocking her. You saw the ring on her finger and you cut off her finger.'

ANATOLY SOLOVYOV, THE VICTIM'S FATHER, TO HER KILLER

Originally, it was Anastasia Solovyova alone who dreamed of settling in America. The beautiful blonde daughter of two music instructors from Bishkek, Kyrgyzstan, excelled at piano and chorus but also studied English assiduously, babysat for an American diplomat in Bishkek and, when she was old enough, joined a bridal agency that would introduce her to American bachelors.

For all of her success in Kyrgyzstan, it was apparent that the 18-year-old ethnic Russian felt that she could build a better life by leaving the former Soviet republic and heading for the United States.

So, when the mail-order bride agency delivered a squat, balding man of almost 40, both she and her parents optimistically saw Gifford Indle King Jr for his finer qualities: intelligent, attentive, well dressed, and he spoke glowingly of his upper-middle-class life and family back in America.

After a few meetings, the Solovyov family was sold.

In their small apartment in Bishkek, Anastasia's parents had no way of knowing that their future son-in-law was actually bisexual, a financial and emotional failure, a man with a history of relying on his well-to-do parents for money and a proclivity for violent relationships. Nor could they have conceived that, just a few years earlier, he had been divorced by Yekaterina Kazakova, another mail-order bride whose court petition alleged that he had hit her in the head with his fist, thrown her against a wall and repeatedly pounded her head against it.

Unaware of King's previous history with international marriage, Anastasia Solovyova soon left Bishkek for a comfortable townhouse just north of Seattle. 'At first she seemed happy. She thought she loved him,' said Natasha Jankauskas, 22, who worked with Anastasia King at a downtown Seattle seafood restaurant soon after she arrived in America. 'But they were never suited for each other… She was tall, beautiful and outgoing, and her husband was very monotone and pretty unattractive.'

After a few months, the couple's problems exceeded mere incompatibility. 'He started getting frustrated with her,' Natasha remembered. 'And then it got to the point where Anastasia came into work crying one day because he had smacked her during a driving lesson.'

Yet Natasha, a music teacher, later described Anastasia as 'amazingly hard-working' and a 'universal favourite, constantly surrounded by friends. She persevered and even thrived in America'.

Anastasia studied with determination when she wasn't working as a restaurant hostess and within two years gained admittance to the prestigious University of Washington, where she intended to study law.

At the same time, she appeared to be bracing for her own legal battle. She began keeping a diary and journals to document the increasingly dysfunctional relationship with her husband, and eventually stored them in a safety deposit box at a local bank, away from his controlling eye.

According to court documents, the diary detailed 'instances where [Anastasia King] was the victim of domestic violence, invasion of privacy and sexual assault'. It also included mentions of her ensuing disgust with her husband and evidence of her own extramarital affairs.

Indle King filed for divorce in 2000. In September of that year, Anastasia visited her parents in Kyrgyzstan and then flew back to Seattle, but never returned to work. Co-workers reported her missing on 2 October. Then, on 28 December, police found her body wrapped in a dog blanket and buried in a shallow grave at a scrapyard on the Tulalip Indian reservation north of Seattle. But, just when Anastasia's already stunned family and friends were expecting murder charges to be filed in Snohomish County Superior Court against her husband, the investigation began to focus on Daniel Kristopher Larson, a 20-year-old registered sex offender who himself had rented a room briefly at the Kings' home.

It was Larson who first brought investigators to Anastasia King's body, after he claimed that Indle King had made a confession to him. However, further questioning led them to conclude that Larson himself had strangled her while her 270-pound husband pinned her down. Furthermore, investigators said, one of the reasons for the murder was that Anastasia had discovered that Larson and her husband were lovers.

At King's trial, Anastasia's father shook his finger at the killer and berated him in Russian for his cruelty. 'You dragged her to the grave you dug... You stripped her corpse, mocking her. You saw the ring on her finger and you cut off her finger. What cruelty! You placed her body face down into the dirt – your beloved wife. An ordinary person cannot even imagine it.'

Because Larson was already in jail for soliciting sex with a 16-year-old Ukrainian girl, prosecutors had worried that he was an unreliable witness. Anastasia King's funeral took place in Seattle on Saturday, 3 February 2003, at St Nicolas's Cathedral on Capitol Hill. Her grave is under a young evergreen tree in a local cemetery.

Whatever the specifics of why, how or even who committed the crime, people agree that the woman from Kyrgyzstan was ultimately a victim of the leap of faith her family took to help her find a new life in the USA.

Ironically, in the process of trying to come to terms with their grief in this faraway country, Anastasia's father, 63, and mother, 55, had also fallen under America's spell. At the end of two weeks which had included gruelling interviews with the prosecution, at a tearful Orthodox memorial service for their daughter the grieving couple held what was to be their final press conference. 'I hope,' Anatoly Solovyov told the assembled reporters wearily, 'that authorities will find a possibility to allow us to remain here for the rest of our lives.'

On 23 March 2002, Larson was sentenced to 20 years in prison and King to 29 years.

The case of Anastasia Solovyova was not the first internet-related homicide to visit Seattle.

Susanna Blackwell met her husband through an internet marriage agency and in 1994 left her native Philippines to move to Washington State to marry him. During their short marriage, Timothy Blackwell regularly abused his wife physically and within a few months she had left him and begun divorce proceedings. The couple had been separated for more than a year when Timothy Blackwell learned that Susanna was eight months pregnant with another man's child. On the last day of the divorce proceedings, he shot and killed Susanna, her unborn child and two friends who were waiting outside the Seattle courtroom.

JOHN E ROBINSON: BODIES IN BARRELS

Among serial killers, John E Robinson is unique. During a career of trawling for victims, this murderer graduated from newspaper personal ads to the internet with homicidal results, earning in the process the distinction of becoming the first cyber serial murderer.

Robinson's case exposed a strange and dangerous secret world of bondage and sadomasochistic sex – one that is flourishing in chatrooms and on other websites today.

But who is this man? Where did he come from and what were the circumstances that brought him the notoriety he so richly deserves? John E Robinson, known to his friends as JR, was born on Monday, 27 December 1943, in Cicero, Illinois, a working-class suburb of Chicago.

One of five children in a devout Roman Catholic family, John grew up at 4916 West 32nd Street. His father, Henry, worked as a machinist for Western Electric and, although respectable enough, was given to occasional bouts of heavy drinking.

By all accounts, John's mother, Alberta, was the backbone of the family and ensured that the couple's five offspring had a decent upbringing.

At 13, John became an Eagle Scout and in November 1957 was chosen as the leader of 120 Scouts who flew to London to appear before the Queen at the Palladium theatre. A popular boy, he had an engaging smile that seems to have served him well.

At 21, he married Nancy Jo Lynch and moved to Kansas City, where Dr Wallace Graham employed John as a lab technician and office manager. Dr Graham was, for many years, the personal physician to no less eminent a patient than the former US President Harry S Truman.

Robinson began his criminal activities in 1967, but he soon came unstuck and was placed on probation for three years. He had embezzled $33,000 from Dr Graham. A spell of probation did not deter the young man, who, after becoming a manager in a TV rental business, started stealing merchandise from his new employer. The company fired him, but did not prosecute.

Over the next decade, Robinson – of whom one employer said he 'gave a very good impression, well dressed, nice looking... seemed to know a lot, very glib and a good speaker' – was often in trouble with the police. He defrauded tens of thousands of dollars from companies who took him on, and set up his own bogus businesses to help him along the way. But, despite being on parole for most of the time, he still managed to prosper.

In 1977, Robinson bought a large house set in four acres in Pleasant Valley Farms, an affluent and prosperous neighbourhood in Johnson County, Kansas. By now, he and Nancy had four children and it was here, in picturesque, rural surroundings, that the confidence trickster and embezzler formed another company, Hydro-Gro Inc, which dealt in hydroponics.

His own publicity material, a 64-page brochure, portrayed him as a sought-after lecturer and author and 'one of the nation's pioneers in indoor home hydroponics'. He managed somehow to engineer his appointment to the board of governors of a workshop for disabled people. He had been involved with the workshop for scarcely more than two months when he was named 'Man of the Year' for his work with handicapped people. Amid much publicity, the *Kansas City Times* proclaimed Robinson's virtues and, at a special dinner and presentation ceremony, he was given a grandiose gesture of approbation in the form of a certificate signed by the mayor.

A short time later, however, the meritorious award was exposed as having been obtained fraudulently. It had been granted as a result of faked letters of commendation received at City Hall, all written by none other than 'Man of the Year' himself, John E Robinson.

Nevertheless, in 1980 Robinson was given the position of director of personnel by another company, and very soon he homed in, like a heat-seeking missile, on his employers' money, directing some of it into his own bank account. After diverting $40,000 to PSA, a company he owned, he yet again found himself placed on probation, this time for five years.

Undaunted by this latest setback, Robinson founded yet another firm, Equi-Plus, to add to his impressive portfolio. This newcomer to the Robinson stable specialised in management consultancy and was very soon engaged by Back Care Systems, a company which ran seminars on the treatment of back pain.

Equi-Plus was asked to prepare a package that included a marketing plan, printed publicity material and videos. However, what the company actually provided was a string of inflated, and in some cases bogus, invoices. Once again, a criminal investigation was begun into the business activities of John Robinson, who responded by producing a series of faked affidavits, all of which attested to the legitimacy of the invoices.

While the investigation continued, Robinson founded Equi-II and it was while at the helm of this new outfit that he moved into a sphere of activities far more sinister than fraud and embezzlement.

With the $40,000 of stolen funds, JR acquired an apartment in Olathe, a town to the south of Kansas City. Here he was able to enjoy sexual affairs with two women, one of whom is quoted as saying, 'John kind of swept me off my feet. He treated me like a queen and always had money to take me to nice restaurants and hotels.'

But there is no such thing as a free lunch, and retribution loomed on the horizon for the thieving and libidinous Robinson. The theft of the money resulted in his being convicted and, given his criminal record, this time he faced a possible prison sentence of seven years. However, he escaped with having to spend only a couple of months behind bars and once more found himself placed on probation for five years.

In 1984, an attractive young woman named Paula Godfrey went to work for JR at Equi-II. She was told by her new boss that she was going to be sent to Texas to attend a training course paid for by the company. Robinson collected Paula from her parents' home in Overland Park, a southern suburb of Kansas City, to drive her to the airport.

Her family never saw her again.

Having heard nothing from their daughter for several days, Paula's parents became anxious and eventually contacted the police to report her missing. The police questioned Robinson, but when he professed ignorance of Paula's whereabouts they went away satisfied with what he had told them. Not long afterwards, the police received a letter bearing Paula Godfrey's signature which began: 'By the time you read this I'll be long gone. I haven't decided on Cleveland, Chicago or Denver, oh well.' In the rest of the letter, Paula seemed to be saying that she was perfectly fine but didn't want to remain in touch with her family.

After reading the letter, the police closed their investigation. It is now widely believed that Paula Godfrey was JR's first murder victim, as she has never been seen again.

In pursuit of his new vocation as a philanthropic helper of young women, JR approached the Truman Medical Center, a Kansas City hospital. There he spoke to social workers, telling them that he, together with some other local businessmen, had formed Kansas City Outreach. This was a charitable organisation, he said, which would provide young unmarried mothers with housing and career training, along with a babysitting service. He pitched the same story to Birthright, an organisation which gave help to young pregnant women.

According to the writer David McClintick, JR told both organisations that Outreach was likely to receive 'funding from Xerox, IBM and other major corporations'. In any event, the great philanthropist asked the social workers to submit candidates who they felt would be suitable for the Outreach programme and in early January 1985 he was contacted by the Truman Medical Center and put in touch with Lisa Stasi.

Nineteen-year-old Lisa had a daughter of four months named Tiffany. Her marriage had fallen apart and Carl Stasi had left his wife and baby to join the US Navy.

Lisa and Tiffany were staying at Hope House, a shelter for battered women, when JR, using the name John Osborne, arrived on the scene, offering her free accommodation and career training. He explained to Lisa that this involved helping her to gain her High School Equivalency Diploma, after which he would arrange for her to go to Texas to train as a silkscreen printer. After she had completed her training, he said, there would be job opportunities for her in Chicago, Denver or Kansas City. In the meantime, her new mentor told her, he would not only pay for her accommodation and living expenses but also give her a monthly stipend of $800.

It was an offer she couldn't refuse.

The kindly benefactor then took Lisa and Tiffany from the refuge and installed them in Room 131 at the Rodeway Inn, a motel in Overland Park, telling her that she and her baby would be travelling to Chicago within a few days. He then got her to sign four blank sheets of notepaper and provide him with the addresses of her immediate family, saying that, as she would be too busy to write letters when she got to Chicago, he would write them for her, to let her relatives know her whereabouts. When JR had left the motel, Lisa went to see some relatives in Kansas City to discuss the matter with them.

On 9 January, JR collected Lisa and the baby from her sister-in-law's home. After expressing anger that she had checked out of the motel, he insisted that they leave with him immediately and so they drove off in a heavy snowstorm.

Like Paula Godfrey, Lisa Stasi was never again seen by her family.

The following evening, JR's brother Don and his wife Helen turned up at JR's home. The childless couple had been trying to adopt a baby for some years, and now JR said he could help them. He explained that the baby's mother had committed suicide at a women's shelter and, for a cash sum of $5,000 and their signatures on a bogus adoption certificate, JR handed Tiffany Stasi over to them.

According to testimony given by Nancy Robinson years later, JR had brought the baby home the previous night, 9 January 1985. She recalled that it was snowing heavily when her husband arrived home and that the infant was not very clean. Apart from some spare nappies, the baby had only the clothes she was wearing, and some baby food.

Don and Helen Robinson were delighted with their new child, whom they named Heather. It would be 15 years before Heather's true identity was revealed, and then in the most shocking circumstances: the man she knew as 'Uncle John' would stand in court accused of murdering her mother.

At the time that Lisa and Tiffany Stasi disappeared, Ann Smith, an employee of Birthright, began to check up on the details that Robinson had provided concerning Kansas City Outreach. They were false. Deeply concerned, she contacted two FBI agents, Thomas Lavin and Jeffrey Dancer, who were assigned to investigate JR and teamed up with his probation officer, Stephen Haymes.

Among the information that began to emerge about JR was the fact that Johnson County's district attorney was investigating Equi-II in connection with strong allegations that it had defrauded its client Back Care Systems. Not only that but JR and a fellow ex-convict, Irvin Blattner, were being investigated by the US Secret Service for forgery involving a government cheque.

None of this, however, was connected to the disappearances of the two women and the baby, and the trail in this direction was in danger of growing cold.

Although everything seemed to point to JR's having abducted and murdered two women, the two FBI investigators and Haymes could do little, despite their own strong suspicions. Nevertheless, Haymes ordered JR to attend his office for further questioning. During the interview, the wily Robinson protested about being harangued over the matter and insisted that Lisa and the baby were, in fact, alive and well. He claimed that a woman who lived in the Kansas City area, for whom Lisa had recently done some babysitting, had told him this. However, when agent Lavin questioned the woman, she confessed that her statement that Lisa had babysat for her was untrue. She said that Robinson had made her go along with the story because she owed him money and he had photographed her nude in order to promote her services as a prostitute.

With this new angle to pursue, the FBI men arranged for a female agent to pose as a prostitute and approach JR on the pretext of looking for work.

According to David McClintick, it was around this time that Robinson developed a taste for sadomasochistic sex. However, not only did he himself engage in S&M, but he also saw its potential to make a lot of money, and very soon he was running a thriving business exploiting this lucrative sector of the sex market. He organised a string of prostitutes to cater for customers who enjoyed S&M. To look after his own appetites, JR employed a male stripper, nicknamed M&M, to find suitable women for him.

The female FBI agent was wired, to record any conversation, and arranged to meet JR at a restaurant in Overland Park. Over lunch, JR explained to her that, working as a prostitute for him, she could earn up to $3,000 for a weekend travelling to Denver or Dallas to service wealthy clients. She could also make $1,000 a night just working in the Kansas City area. His clients, he said, were drawn mainly from the ranks of doctors, lawyers and judges.

JR went on to explain that, as an S&M prostitute, the young woman would have to allow herself to be subjected to painful treatment, such as having her nipples manipulated with pliers. When they heard this part of the recording of the conversation, the FBI investigation team decided to end the undercover operation out of fear for their agent's safety. It is doubtful that the woman herself would have been enthusiastic to continue after hearing about that aspect of the job.

Robinson maintained an apartment on Troost Avenue in Overland Park and it was here that he installed a girl named Theresa Williams in April 1985. Twenty-one and attractive, Theresa had been introduced to JR by M&M as a suitable candidate for prostitution. She had been working at various odd jobs around Kansas City and jumped at the chance. After photographing her nude in a hotel room, JR initially offered her a position as his mistress. This involved her being given an apartment with all her expenses paid, and for her there was the added attraction that JR would keep her well provided with amphetamines and marijuana. She would also be expected to provide sexual services for others, for which she would receive prostitution fees. Theresa took the job and moved into the Troost Avenue apartment.

But life for Theresa wasn't all roses. One night towards the end of April, after being given $1,200 and a new outfit by JR, she was taken, blindfold in a limousine, to a mansion. There she was introduced to a distinguished-looking man of about 60, who led her down to a basement which was fitted out as a medieval torture chamber. Her host instructed her to remove all her clothes and moments later she found herself being stretched on a rack. Theresa panicked and demanded to be allowed to leave. Blindfolded again, she was driven back to her apartment. JR reacted angrily and a few days later she had to give back the $1,200.

On another occasion, JR took her to task for entertaining a boyfriend at the apartment. However, the worst was yet to come. In late May, JR paid her a visit during which he did something that caused her more fear than she had ever known in her life. She was asleep when he let himself into the apartment. He burst into the bedroom, dragged her out of bed by her hair and spanked her until she began to scream. After throwing her to the floor, JR drew a revolver, put it to her head and pulled the trigger. Instead of an explosion, there was only a click. The chamber was empty.

By now, Theresa was whimpering with fear, but she went rigid with utter terror as JR slid the revolver slowly down her stomach and inserted the barrel into her vagina. He left it there for several terrifying seconds before withdrawing it, replacing it in its holster and, without another word, leaving the apartment.

About a week after the incident with the gun, Lavin and Dancer called unannounced at Theresa's apartment. Having been told that they were investigating the disappearance of two women and that JR was the suspect, she decided to reveal the truth. That, of course, involved telling them about the drugs that JR was supplying to her as well as the incident with the gun. When the agents learned that Theresa had been asked by JR to sign some blank sheets of notepaper, they felt they had reason to believe that her life was in danger, and moved her to a secret location.

Together with Stephen Haymes, the agents filed a report with the Missouri court which claimed that Robinson had violated his probation conditions by carrying a gun and supplying drugs to Theresa Williams. They asked the court to revoke his probation and put him in prison.

Once more, however, JR avoided imprisonment on a technicality: his lawyer argued successfully that, because he had not been allowed to confront his accuser, Theresa Williams, his constitutional rights had been violated. However, his real-estate fraud case, in Johnson County, ended with his being sentenced to serve between six and 19 years.

Around the time that JR was about to go to prison, the police were searching for 27-year-old Catherine Clampitt. Born in Korea but adopted and raised by the Bales family in Texas, Catherine was a one-time drug user now seeking rehabilitation. She had begun to work for JR at Equi-II in early 1987, but had disappeared a few months later. Despite the fact that in some quarters suspicion of murder once again fell on Robinson, no further action was taken against him.

Strangely, JR took to the prison regime like a duck takes to water. He was the model inmate, making such a good impression on the prison authorities that the parole board set him free in January 1991, after he had served just four years.

However, he still had to go to jail in Missouri for having violated the terms of his probation resulting from the $40,000 fraud he had perpetrated more than a decade earlier. He went back behind bars for a further two years.

It is interesting to read Stephen Haymes's assessment of Robinson in a memo that he wrote to a colleague in 1991. It says, 'I believe him to be a con-man out of control. He leaves in his wake many unanswered questions and missing persons... I have observed Robinson's sociopathic tendencies, habitual criminal behaviour, inability to tell the truth and scheming to cover his own actions at the expense of others.' The probation officer went on to say, 'I was not surprised to see he had a good institution adjustment [settled in well] in Kansas considering that he is quite bright and a white-collar con-man capable of being quite personable and friendly to those around him.'

While in jail in Missouri, the 'white-collar con-man' forged a friendship with the prison doctor, William Bonner. He also developed a relationship with Bonner's wife, Beverly. She was the prison librarian and JR very soon found that he had a job in the library.

On the outside, Nancy Robinson had found the going tough without her husband's income and eventually had had to sell their palatial home at Pleasant Valley Farms. What is more, she had had to take a job to keep body and soul together and she was fortunate in getting one that provided accommodation. She became the manager of a mobile-home development in

Belton, a suburb of Kansas City on the Missouri side of the state line.

It was to these modest quarters that JR went when he was released from prison early in 1993. The two older children had grown up and left home and the twins were at college, so JR and Nancy had the place to themselves. They rented storage lockers near by to house their surplus belongings.

JR set to work restoring the family fortunes. There was never any real likelihood that he would stay on the straight and narrow and it wasn't long before he was back to his old ways.

By now, Beverly Bonner had left her husband and begun divorce proceedings. A few months later, she moved to Kansas City and went to work with JR, who appointed her a director of his company Hydro-Gro.

Not long after this grand appointment, Beverly's alimony cheques were finding their way into an Olathe post-office box number used by Robinson.

Beverly Bonner was not seen or heard from after January 1994.

JR's next victim was a widow named Sheila Dale Faith. When her husband, John, died of cancer in 1993, Sheila was left to bring up their teenage daughter, Debbie.

Debbie was born with spina bifida and spent her life in a wheelchair. Life was not easy for the two, who had moved from California to live in Pueblo, Colorado, and depended on Social Security payments.

It isn't certain exactly how Sheila met JR, although it may have been through a newspaper ad, but, after being in Pueblo for only a few months, she and Debbie moved to Kansas City. Sheila told her friends that she had met her 'dream man', John, who had promised to take her on a cruise. He had also assured her that she would never have to work or worry about taking care of Debbie, as he would look after them both; money was no problem.

One night in the summer of 1994, with no prior warning, JR called at Sheila's home and she and Debbie were taken away by him to live in 'the Kansas City area'.

As was the case with so many other women who were befriended by JR, the two Faiths were never seen again.

Sheila Faith had been receiving disability benefits from the Social Security Administration for herself and Debbie. Now these payments were being sent to a mail centre in Olathe, where they were collected by Robinson. In the autumn of 1994, according to court documents, Robinson filed a medical report to the Social Security Administration. In the report, he claimed that Debbie was 'totally disabled' and would require care for the rest of her life. The report, however, bore the signature of William Bonner, the doctor with whom J.R had been friendly when he was in prison and who until recently had been Beverly Bonner's husband. When he was eventually questioned on the matter, Dr Bonner denied ever having met Sheila or Debbie Faith, and had certainly never treated either.

In any event, JR collected the Faiths' disability cheques for almost six years.

In July 2000, Cass County Prosecutors alleged that, between 1994 and 1997, Robinson had defrauded the US Government of more than $29,000 in Social Security and disability payments by forging documents to suggest that Sheila and Debbie Faith were alive.

It was also alleged that he received more than $14,000 in alimony cheques that should have gone to Beverly Bonner. The owner of the mail centre from which Robinson retrieved the cheques told police that he knew JR as James Turner.

JR's interest in sadomasochistic sex continued to flourish and he began placing adverts in the personal columns of a Kansas City newspaper named *Pitch Weekly*. Chloe Elizabeth, a businesswomen from Topeka, Kansas, claimed that JR sent her a wealth of publicity material selected to show him in a good light. He included newspaper clippings describing his appearance before the Queen when he was a Boy Scout, his hydroponics brochure, details of his Man of the Year award and a Kansas University brochure containing pictures of two of his children. It was altogether an odd portfolio for someone wishing to engage in a BDSM encounter – the term widely used to describe relationships involving bondage and sadomasochism. Unsurprisingly, JR's lengthy and distinguished criminal record received no mention whatsoever.

In later years, Chloe Elizabeth described an event that took place during the afternoon of 25 October 1995. 'I was to meet him at the door wearing only a sheer robe, black mesh thong panties, a matching demi-cup bra, stockings and black high heels. My eyes were to be made up dark and lips red. I was to kneel before him,' she recounted.

On arriving, JR took a leather-studded collar from his pocket, placed it around her neck and attached a long leash to the collar. After a drink and some small talk, he made Chloe Elizabeth remove all her clothes except for her stockings, and then took from his pocket a 'Contract for Slavery' in which she consented to let him use her as a sexual toy in any way he saw fit.

'I read the contract and signed it. He asked if I was sure. I said yes, very sure,' said Chloe Elizabeth.

After he had tied her to the bed, whipped her and carried out a variety of acts on her breasts with ropes and nipple clamps, JR concluded their first date by making her perform oral sex on him. Chloe Elizabeth was delighted with her new master and he was pretty much delighted with her.

'That was the first date. It was sensational! He had the ability to command, to control, to corral someone as strong and aggressive and spirited as I am,' she said.

Before he left, JR told Chloe Elizabeth that she had been stupid for allowing him to do everything he had done to her. 'I could have killed you,' he said.

However, Chloe Elizabeth was not as naive as he may have thought. Without his knowledge, she had taken the sensible precaution of having a male friend stationed in another room of her house, listening vigilantly for any sound of excessive behaviour. The man also noted down the number of JR's car.

The relationship between Chloe Elizabeth and JR burgeoned and they were meeting at least twice a week before it waned as she started to find out that Robinson was not all he claimed to be.

It is not unusual in BDSM relationships for the dominant partner to take control of the submissive partner's assets and financial affairs, an arrangement that is sometimes included in the contract drawn up between slave and master. Naturally, given his passion for other people's money, JR broached this issue with Chloe Elizabeth and suggested that they exchange lists of their assets. She, wisely, refused, suspecting that he was after her money. Knowing as we do now that he was merely the unemployed husband of a woman who was the manager of a mobile-home park, it would be interesting to see just what those assets were that JR had intended listing, apart from Beverly Bonner's alimony cheques and the Faiths' welfare payments.

If JR had imagined that Chloe Elizabeth's submissiveness extended beyond her sexual inclinations, he was badly mistaken; she was an intelligent and successful businesswoman, not an ill-educated teenage mother desperate for help and support. Their relationship was by now moving in the wrong direction as she found out more and more about him.

He told her that he was going to Australia and would be away for some time. However, she discovered that he had not even left Kansas. When she telephoned his office, the phone was answered but remained utterly silent. About an hour afterwards, her phone rang and she found herself being berated by a furious JR. He accused her of checking up on him and warned her in very unpleasant tones against that sort of behaviour.

The final straw for Chloe Elizabeth was when she found out about JR's criminal record, and in February 1996 she ended their relationship.

That same year, the Robinsons left the mobile-home park and went to live over on the Kansas side of the border, near Olathe. The development that they moved to was called the Santa Barbara Estates, where again Nancy worked as estate manager.

Their new address was 36 Monterey, and here they certainly didn't opt for inconspicuous anonymity. They erected a statue of St Francis of Assisi in the yard at the front of their home, hung wind chimes at their front door and at Christmas earned quite a reputation for their spectacular display of decorations.

As well as their home on the Santa Barbara Estates, JR and Nancy bought some farmland near the small town of La Cygne, south of Olathe. They had about 16 acres of land that also contained a fishing pond to which JR invited friends from time to time. The couple improved the place by putting a mobile home and a shed on the site.

In pursuit of his sexual preferences, JR had by now left personal ads behind and embraced the internet. Using the handle 'Slavemaster', he maintained five computers and spent hours trawling BDSM sites. Ultimately, it would be two of his internet contacts who would be instrumental in bringing his world crashing around his ears, but in 1996 that was still some years ahead.

The following year, Robinson encountered a young, Polish-born undergraduate on the internet. Her name was Izabel Lewicka and she was studying fine arts at Purdue University in Indiana.

Izabel's parents were very concerned when, in the spring of 1997, she told them that she was moving to Kansas, having been offered an internship. She wasn't forthcoming with details, doing nothing to allay her parents' misgivings other than leave an address on Metcalf Avenue in Overland Park. In June, she left Purdue and drove off to Kansas. Her parents were never to see her again.

After receiving no reply to their letters, the Lewickas grew extremely anxious about their daughter and in August drove to Kansas to find out what was the matter. They arrived to find that the address on Metcalf Avenue was simply a mailbox; their daughter didn't live there. When they asked the manager of the place for Izabel's forwarding address, he refused to divulge the information. Despite their anxiety, Izabel's parents did not bother to contact the police but returned to Indiana.

Izabel was, in fact, still alive at that time and living a life far removed from the one she had known in Indiana. And she had good reason to keep it a secret from her parents. Her new friend JR had provided her with an apartment in south Kansas City and there they enjoyed a BDSM relationship. They even had a 'slave contract' which contained more than 100 clauses governing their conduct, she as the slave and he as the master.

In return for her submission, JR maintained Izabel financially, paying all her bills. When she wasn't engaged in sexual activity with him, Izabel enjoyed the life of a lady of leisure. Her main interest was reading gothic and vampire novels bought from a specialist bookshop in Overland Park that she visited frequently. But she didn't abandon her studies completely, for in the autumn of 1998, using the surname Lewicka-Robinson, Izabel enrolled at Johnson County Community College. Her adoption of JR's surname lends weight to reports which concluded that the young woman believed they were going to marry. In any event, in January 1999, a few months after her enrolment at the college, JR moved Izabel into another apartment, in Olathe. This was closer to his own home, which may account for his sometimes describing her as a graphic designer employed by his company Specialty Publications. On occasion, however, he is known to have referred to her as his adopted daughter, while at other times he described her as his niece.

Then Izabel Lewicka disappeared and was never heard from again.

Slavemaster soon returned to the world of sadomasochistic chatrooms and made contact with Suzette Trouten, a 27-year-old nurse from Newport, Michigan.

Suzette, whose non-sexual interests were collecting teapots and doting on her two Pekinese, pursued a highly active BDSM lifestyle, carrying on relationships with as many as four dominants at once.

She had pierced not only her nipples and navel but also five places in and around her genitals, all to accommodate rings and other devices used in BDSM rituals. A photograph of Suzette, with nails driven through her breasts, had been circulated on the internet. She certainly appealed to JR and soon a relationship developed.

In fact, JR was so enamoured of his new, submissive friend that he concocted a very attractive job offer to entice her to fly down from Michigan for an interview. He paid for her flight, and when she arrived at Kansas City there was a limousine at the airport to meet her.

The job, he told her, involved being a companion and nurse to his very rich, elderly father, who travelled a lot but needed constant care. He went on to say that his father did most of his travelling on a yacht and that her duties would involve her sailing with them between California and Hawaii. For this, she would be paid a salary of $60,000 and be provided with an apartment and a car. He neglected to mention that the only way to have contact with his father would be through the use of a Ouija board, or a medium, as the old man had been dead for some ten years. But JR was not a man to let such details inhibit his designs and he gave Suzette to understand that the interview had gone well and the job was hers. She returned to

Michigan and began putting her affairs in order before relocating to Kansas.

While she was making ready to move, Suzette spoke to her mother, Carolyn, to whom she was very close, telling her all about her new job. She also discussed it with Lori Remington, a Canadian friend; they had met in a chatroom and shared an interest in BDSM. Later, she introduced Lori to JR on the internet and they too developed a long-distance, dominant–submissive, cyber relationship.

In February 2000, Suzette rented a truck, loaded it with her belongings and headed off to her new life in Kansas City. She took with her clothes, books, her collection of teapots and the two Pekinese, along with her array of BDSM accessories, including whips and paddles.

Lenexa is a suburb of Kansas City, lying west of Overland Park and north of Olathe, and it was there that Robinson took Suzette, when she arrived on 14 February. He had reserved accommodation for her, Room 216, at the Guesthouse Suites, an extended-stay hotel, and arranged for her dogs, Peka and Harry, to be boarded at the kennels of Ridgeview Animal Hospital in Olathe. They would be able to go with her on the yacht, he explained, but the Guesthouse Suites didn't allow dogs.

Almost immediately after Suzette had settled in, JR told her to get herself a passport, as they would be leaving in a fortnight. He also produced a 'master–slave' contract covering their BDSM activities, which she duly signed. Then, ominously, he got her to attach her signature to 30 sheets of blank paper and to address more than 40 envelopes to relatives and some of her friends. Just as he had done with other women, he told Suzette that he would take care of her correspondence while they were travelling, as she would be too busy to do so herself.

Suzette was the youngest of a family of five children and, according to Carolyn Trouten, 'She was a kind of a mama's girl.' While she was in Kansas, she phoned her mother every day, keeping her informed of how things were going and, although she had at first worried that she would be homesick, she seemed to be in good spirits and was certainly happy with her employer, John Robinson. And he was, evidently, happy with her.

On 1 March, Carolyn spoke to her daughter, who was looking forward to her impending yacht cruise with her wealthy boss and his father, and Suzette promised to phone her regularly.

Then Suzette simply disappeared. After not having spoken with her daughter for some time, Carolyn made a few discreet enquiries, then called the police.

Detective David Brown began an immediate and thorough investigation of the man whom he saw as the prime suspect, John Robinson. He obtained JR's criminal record and contacted the Overland Park Police. The rap sheet acquainted him with the other reports of missing women and soon he saw the potential connection. After two detectives had spoken to Stephen Haymes, Robinson's probation officer in Missouri, it became clear that they could possibly be investigating a serial killer.

David Brown instructed the Trouten family and a few other acquaintances of JR's to tape their telephone conversations with JR and to pass to the police copies of all emails from him.

At the time that Suzette had been preparing to move to Kansas, JR, using the name James Turner, had established two more BDSM friendships on the internet. The first woman was a psychologist from Texas who had placed an advert on a BDSM site. She had recently lost her job and when JR became aware of this he promised to help her to find work in the Kansas City area.

Jeanne arrived in Lenexa on 6 April and, while staying at the Guesthouse Suites, spent five days getting to know JR. During that time she signed a contract in which she consented to 'give my body to him in any way he sees fit'. They also discussed her working for Hydro-Gro and JR told her to return home and prepare to move to Kansas City.

Jeanne returned for another long weekend in late April and it was then that she found that JR was eager to pursue more severe and violent forms of bondage sex than she wanted, but as she believed he was going to find work for her she consented to his demands, allowing him to brutalise her far beyond the limits she had intended. She later testified that he took photographs of her while she was bound and nude and hit her hard across the face. 'I had never been slapped that hard by anybody before,' she told the court. She also stressed that the photographs were taken against her wishes and despite her protests.

Fortunately for Jeanne, the promised move to Kansas never took place and she demanded the return of her sex toys, worth more than $500. JR chivalrously refused. Moreover, he threatened to publicly reveal the slave contract and the explicit, compromising photographs.

Jeanne's response was to report the matter to the police.

Kate was the second of the two women, and she turned out to be the last one to fall foul of Slavemaster. She was an accountant and, after some weeks of preamble on the internet, agreed to become Robinson's slave. In mid-May she journeyed to Kansas for a few days with JR and was installed in an apartment at the Guesthouse Suites.

Later, Kate recalled that on Friday, 19 May she received a phone call from Robinson telling her that he would be coming round to see her. During the call he instructed her that when he arrived she was to be kneeling in the corner of the room completely naked with her hair tied back.

Submissive Kate was ready, as instructed, when JR arrived. Yet she wasn't prepared for what actually happened. He walked into the room, grabbed her by her hair and flogged her brutally across her breasts and back. Like Jeanne before her, Kate was discovering that JR was interested in a much rougher relationship than she wanted. She, too, didn't like being photographed during sex, but he insisted on doing so; he seemed excited by recording the marks his beatings made on her body. However, Kate's genuine distaste for that level of treatment must have spoiled his enjoyment, because he told her he didn't like her attitude and wanted to end their relationship. Her body burning and bruised from the flogging, Kate became hysterical and after JR had left she got dressed and made her way in tears to the reception desk. There she asked for the registration card and it was then that she discovered that her host's name was not James Turner but John Robinson. Worried and distraught, she called Lenexa Police, who, on hearing that JR was involved, gave her complaint the utmost priority.

The detective who arrived at the hotel in response to Kate's call was David Brown, who had been investigating Robinson since the disappearance of Suzette Trouten more than two months before. Convinced that JR was a killer, Brown was not going to risk leaving another woman in the position of being a potential victim. When he had heard Kate's tearful story, he got her to collect her belongings together and moved her to another hotel.

The next day, Kate gave a full interview to Detective David Brown. She explained how she had met 'James Turner' via the internet and how she had been invited to Kansas to embark on a master-and-slave relationship. She told him that Robinson had beaten her with a violence far beyond her desires, explaining that she didn't go in for pain and punishment or marks on her skin. 'I'm a submissive, not a masochist,' she said.

The complaints and statements from the two women from Texas, Jeanne and Kate, gave the police the means to justify arresting the man who had been the subject of their investigation into the unexplained disappearances of several women. On Friday, 2 June, nine police cars drove to the Santa Barbara Estates in Olathe, where they surrounded 36 Monterey. There detectives arrested John E. Robinson and charged him with sexual assault – although by the end of the following few days he would willingly have settled for such a simple charge. Visibly shocked, JR was handcuffed and driven away to the Johnson County Jail. At the same time, police and detectives spilled from the eight other cars and began to execute a search warrant for the Robinson home.

Inside, as well as seizing all five of JR's computers, the police found a blank sheet of notepaper which had been signed by Lisa Stasi more than 15 years earlier, in January 1985. Along with this were receipts from the Rodeway Inn in Overland Park which showed that JR had checked Lisa out on 10 January of that year, the day after she and her baby, Tiffany, had last been seen alive by the managers. However, those first scraps of evidence were only the tip of a gigantic iceberg: Far more would come to light over the next few days and it would horrify those who found it.

The police investigation had been thorough and revealed all

property owned or rented by Robinson. Consequently, a second search warrant had been obtained for that morning and, as JR was being driven to jail, detectives were busy searching his storage locker in Olathe. There they found a cornucopia of items connecting him to two of the missing women, Izabel Lewicka and Suzette Trouten. They found Trouten's birth certificate, her Social Security card, several sheets of blank notepaper signed 'Love ya, Suzette' and a slave contract signed by her. Beside Suzette's things, they found Izabel's driving licence, several photographs of her, nude and in bondage, a slave contract and several BDSM sex implements. They also found a stun gun and a pillowcase.

On the following day, Saturday, 3 June, another search warrant was served. This time, the search team descended on the smallholding that the Robinsons owned near La Cygne. They found two 55-gallon metal barrels near a shed and opened one. Inside was the body of a naked woman, head down and immersed in the fluid which had been produced by decomposition of the body.

The detective who opened the barrel, Harold Hughes, a forensic crime-scene investigator, turned his attention to the second barrel and prised open the lid. Inside, he found a pillow and a pillowcase, which he removed, to reveal another body. Again, it was that of a woman, but this one was clothed. Like the first body, this one was immersed in the fluid resulting from its own decomposition. Hughes completed the customary procedures of photographing and fingerprinting the barrels before resealing them and marking them 'Unknown 1' and 'Unknown 2'.

Later that day, Stephen Haymes, Robinson's former probation

officer, was told of the discovery of the bodies. After so many years of suspicion, his judgement of JR was vindicated. He later told David McClintick, 'It confirmed what I had always believed, but the move from theory to reality was chilling.'

At the time that Haymes was learning of Robinson's arrest, the District Attorney for Johnson County, Paul Morrison, was contacting his counterpart in Cass County, across the state line in Missouri, in order to negotiate the issue of another search warrant. Detectives had discovered that JR maintained a locker at the Stor-Mor-For-Less depot in Raymore, a Missouri suburb of Kansas City. Morrison was an influential figure and was given total co-operation in cutting through the red tape inevitable in issues negotiated between two states. As a result of his discussion, he and a group of detectives from Johnson County arrived at the office of Cass County's deputy prosecutor, Mark Tracy, early the next morning. They carried with them the longest affidavit, in support of a search warrant, that Tracy had ever seen. It asserted that Robinson was believed to have killed several women and that it was suspected that evidence connected with the killings was hidden in the storage locker in Raymore; he had paid to rent the locker with a company cheque, in order to conceal his identity.

At 8am on the Monday morning, Tracy served the search warrant at the storage depot and the Johnson County detectives were led to Robinson's locker. Inside was a lot of clutter and the task force spent more than half an hour sifting through it before they saw, hidden at the back, three barrels. Wafting from the barrels came the nauseating, unmistakable smell of decomposing flesh.

As it was virtually certain that the barrels contained dead

bodies, Tracy summoned his boss, Chris Koster, and the state of Missouri assumed immediate control of the crime scene. A new team of police investigators arrived and the locker was emptied of all its contents, save for the three barrels. These were found to be standing on piles of cat litter; obviously a futile attempt by JR to reduce the smell that was emanating from them.

The first barrel was opened, to reveal a light brown sheet, a pair of spectacles and a shoe. When the crime-lab technician had removed the sheet, he took hold of the shoe, only to find that there was a foot inside it and the foot was still attached to a leg. On the assumption that the storage depot wasn't the best place to investigate the barrels and their contents, it was decided to reseal them and take them to the medical examiner's office in Kansas City. This was not as simple as it seemed. There was a very real fear that the bottoms of the barrels might corrode and give way, so a police officer was sent to a nearby Wal-Mart to buy three children's plastic paddling pools and these were slipped underneath the barrels before they were loaded on to a truck.

Back at the medical examiner's office, the barrels were opened and, as expected, each contained the severely decomposed body of a female. Both women had been beaten to death with an instrument, probably a hammer, and had been dead for some years.

The first body was fully clothed. The second was wearing only a T-shirt and in its mouth was a denture which was broken in two. Body three was that of a teenager and was wearing green trousers and a silver beret. Identification was not immediately possible and was going to take some days.

Over in Kansas, in Topeka, the two bodies found on the

Robinson property were identified by a forensic odontologist as those of Izabel Lewicka and Suzette Trouten: both women had very recently been reported as missing and were easier to trace.

A few days later, with the help of another forensic odontologist, two of the bodies that had been found at the storage depot were identified. One was Beverly Bonner and the other was Sheila Faith. Sheila's daughter, Debbie, who suffered from spina bifida, was identified as the third body, by means of a spinal X-ray.

The case against Robinson was beginning to assume a structure, although there was the problem of jurisdiction in relation to which state, Kansas or Missouri, would be responsible for each murder. Eventually, it was resolved that Robinson would be tried first in Kansas and the date was set for 14 January 2002, before being postponed until September of the same year.

Inmate # 00456690 John E Robinson is currently on Death Row, Kansas, although the state has not carried out an execution since 1976. His current photograph and other details can be found on the Kansas Department of Corrections website.

DARLIE LYNN ROUTIER: THE DOG THAT DIDN'T BARK

'Here's a mother who has supposedly been the victim of a violent crime. She has just lost two children, and yet she's out literally dancing on their graves.'

DALLAS COUNTY ASSISTANT DISTRICT ATTORNEY GREG DAVIS, LEAD PROSECUTOR IN THE DARLIE ROUTIER CASE

Often the internet's link with a murder is not that it was trawled to find the victim; instead, it is exploited to rally international support for the convicted killer. Yet, when I see a glossy, constantly updated website dedicated to promoting a Death Row inmate's innocence, I smell a rat. What is the need for this global exposure, and what use are the pleas for support? And, more often than not, donations are welcomed, of course.

These sites are always maintained by the well-intentioned

anti-death penalty lobby, whose campaigning would be better served if they concentrated their efforts on genuine cases. In short, such websites seem redundant to me.

The thousands of people who visit them are mostly not professionals in criminology-related professions, so what of value do they offer in assisting a convicted prisoner to gain his or her freedom? Surely the inmate's own attorneys are capable of presenting a well-balanced legal argument before the appellate courts without all the hysteria these sites bring with them.

As to the internet debate rooms that attach themselves to these cyberspace ventures like clams to a rock, more often than not they simply post the ramblings of the ill-informed.

All such websites, and Darlie Routier's pages are not exempt, publish selective material favouring the prisoners concerned. Rarely, if ever, do they expose the full facts, so they are patently misleading: a smoke-blowing exercise designed to deceive otherwise honest, often gullible people into supporting a cause that has already been lost.

A glance at the self-serving site dedicated to Darlie Routier's case alludes to 'evidence' that can prove this woman's innocence of the stabbing to death of her two young sons. Documents and affidavits sworn by expert witnesses are listed. Case photographs of the badly injured Routier are also posted to gain public sympathy for the loss she has suffered: her freedom and the lives of her two children.

However, on closer scrutiny, the documents and 'evidence' contained within documents are revealed to be all but worthless, and nowhere do we see the horrific truth.

I have studied this website and I can state that there is nothing here that will influence a court of appeal, and it is this – not the general public – that will be the final arbiter. In addition, I will note, in the wider public interest, that, while the pro-Routier camp pours scorn on the police and trial court's actions, the public prosecutor has remained admirably quiet.

But perhaps the website is of some value in that it brings to light many red herrings. For its content and *raison d'etre* confirm the manipulating, scheming persona of Darlie Routier. The woman is the mistress of homicidal *trompe l'oeil*, for, despite her apparent wide-eyed innocent charm, she is one of the most evil and cold-blooded child-killers of modern times.

This is the story of the dog that didn't bark in the night, and it is a fascinating and educational one at that, for it confirms the widespread and perfectly reasonable suspicion that pure evil lurks within the web.

In approaching this case, we should step back and look at the crime in its entirety. However, given that this crime appears to lack a motive, this particular picture of homicide has many components missing; pieces that are invisible to the human eye. Locating them may solve part of the puzzle; interpreting them and fitting them into the empty spaces to complete the picture is altogether another problem.

But this is no daub we will study so intently. The one we are viewing is akin to one of the masterly works of the Dutch graphic artist Escher, who is renowned for his dreamlike spatial illusions and impossible buildings. Like the murderer in this chapter, he was a wizard at deceiving the eye.

The analogy between Escher's mesmerising work and the case of Darlie Routier is apt, because here we have an enterprise that millions of American citizens agreed was complete, only to change their minds after a short time, so that they now argue instead that it is not. The US Criminal Justice system says that the guilty verdict is the genuine article, while a growing body of commentators have had second thoughts and now claim that the prosecution case fooled the eye, with the result that the verdict is a fake.

And it is for this reason that the life of a condemned woman hangs in the balance.

Most of my readers, particularly those with an interest in criminology and the criminal justice and penal systems, will know that many prison inmates, especially those convicted on overwhelming evidence and facing long prison terms, often appeal against their sentences using trivial issues in their attempts to overturn the sentence or have it reduced. They set their warped and deluded minds the task of convincing themselves, as well as one another, that they are innocent. In the end, so convincing are they that they are able to manipulate hordes of people into believing them.

Commentators on the serial killer Kenneth Bianchi, who continues even today to manipulate society, have termed his behaviour 'fly-specking exercises'. Bianchi meticulously dots the 'i's and crosses the 't's, looking for the smallest errors in his frantic yet pathetic efforts to gain his freedom.

We find exactly the same 'fly-specking' behaviour in the case of the cyber spider Darlie Routier.

Her conviction was seemingly watertight. Indeed, so strong was the 'overwhelming evidence' presented by the prosecution that the jury had no reservations whatsoever about finding Routier guilty of first-degree murder and the judge sentenced her to die by lethal injection.

This was a crime that sent shockwaves around the USA, so much so that, following the hysteria generated by the case, three books were written by well-established authors, each unreservedly portraying Darlie Routier as 'the embodiment of evil'. Now, however, dozens of experts, including several who participated as witnesses, a juror and the author of one of the books that condemned Routier, argue she is innocent. Why? Because, by using the internet, she has convinced them, and the websites that support her cause testify to this fact.

Millions of US citizens believe that Darlie Routier is innocent and should be freed at once, after which, no doubt, she will ask for apologies and financial compensation for having been detained for so long.

Twelve days after the deaths of her two young sons, the police arrested Darlie Routier for their murders. The investigating team had no eyewitnesses, no confession, no apparent motive, and the boys' mother had herself apparently been slashed and stabbed during the attack. One knife wound missed her carotid artery by two millimetres; any closer and she would have bled to death.

What investigators did have by way of physical evidence was a trail of drying blood. It started at the murder scene on the ground floor of the opulent family home and led through a utility room to a mesh window screen in the garage, where it mysteriously stopped.

Other than a knife-slashed window screen – the damage most certainly not sufficient to allow an intruder easy ingress and egress – there was no other possible entry point in the Routiers' house. There were no signs of forcible entry at any of the other doors and windows, 'all of which were secured and locked', according to Routier's husband, Darin.

This fact naturally gave rise to two theories: either the killer had a key to the house or garage, or the murderer was a member of the family. If the second was the case, only the mother or father, or the two together, could have murdered the two children.

The other significant physical evidence was a bloodstained butcher knife on which were Darlie Routier's fingerprints. There were three mysterious fingerprints that couldn't be traced to any individual whatsoever, and Luminol tests for the presence of blood showed that someone had tried to clean the washbasin in the utility room/kitchenette and a settee in the adjoining recreation room – where the children had been slain.

Finally, it was clear that the attacker had used a serrated bread knife from a drawer, but more about this later.

Almost immediately investigators were puzzled and started asking themselves a number of questions.

What was the motive for the murders?

If it was a robbery, why were Darlie's jewellery and purse left untouched?

Why would an intruder kill two children before trying to kill an adult who posed a more serious threat?

The two boys were stabbed in the chest. Why did Darlie Routier suffer a neck wound and cuts on her forearm and shoulder?

Why would the killer, who obviously had no scruples about murdering a pair of small boys, back off when Darlie awoke, leaving a witness alive to identify him?

Why would he drop the murder weapon on the floor, giving Darlie, his pursuer, a weapon with which to fight back?

Why would he have used the Routiers' butcher's knife in the

first place? (Most assailants come to their intended victim's premises already armed.)

Why were there no visible signs of an intruder having entered the house?

And, as the questions mounted, it appeared that a bread knife owned by the Routiers might have been used to cut the garage's screen. Had the intruder used this bread knife to slash his way in? If so, how did he get the knife in the first place?

However, there was one question police did not ask themselves at the time, and apparently not one of the tens of thousands of Routier's supporters has asked this question since. The Routiers owned a white Pomeranian, a yappy little dog, easily excitable, that barked at any visitors to the premises. Deserving of a damn good kick, it even snapped and tore at a police officer's trousers as he walked through the house. The dog was also heard barking by the emergency dispatcher who took Darlie's 911 call, so we know that the animal was around when the frenzied murders took place.

In considering this fact, my mind turns to Arthur Conan Doyle's novel *The Adventure of Silver Blaze*:

Inspector Gregory: 'Is there any other point to which you would wish to draw my attention?'

Sherlock Holmes: 'To the curious incident of the dog in the night-time.'

Inspector Gregory: 'The dog did nothing in the night-time.'

Sherlock Holmes: 'That was the curious incident.'

And here we sniff our first red herring, for it is entirely reasonable to ask: why did the Routiers' dog not bark in the night?

Following two contradictory statements by Darlie Routier, who claimed she was attacked by a black man who left via the garage, the police soon concluded that there had been no intruder that night because everything pointed to the crime scene having been staged.

Doctors who treated Mrs Routier's injuries formed the opinion that they were self-inflicted, and the investigators' suspicions were reinforced by a peculiar scene that was caught on videotape a few days after the double murder.

On 14 June, just nine days after the killings and on what would have been Devon Routier's seventh birthday, Darlie drove to the cemetery with family and friends, wished her boy a happy birthday and then, in a joyous mood, sprayed Silly String all over the fresh mound of earth.

'Here's a mother who has supposedly been the victim of a violent crime,' said Dallas County Assistant District Attorney Greg Davis, the lead prosecutor in the case. 'She has just lost two children, and yet she's out literally dancing on their graves.'

Within eight months of the crime, Darlie was convicted and sentenced to death by a jury in the Kerr County town of Kerrville, where the trial had been moved because of a welter of media hype and publicity. She seemed destined to be remembered as yet another stressed-out mother who had suddenly spiralled out of control. But over the years numerous news stories and an ongoing investigation by Darlie's appellate attorneys have raised questions about what really happened that night.

Could it be that the police and the prosecutors manipulated

Armin Meiwes was the cannibal from Germany.
Top left: Brandes was killed by Meiwes in March 2001, who chopped up and froze what flesh he didn't use in one sitting for later feasts.

Top right: Judge Ruth Rissing-van Saan was the presiding judge in the April 2005 hearing which ordered a retrial of Meiwes. Prosecuters had appealed against his eight-and-a-half year sentence.

Bottom: the house which he shared with his mother for many years and later the location for the meal he made of his guest Bernd-Jurgen Brandes.

Armin Meiwes in court in January 2004. The gruesome story of how he ate Brandes' penis inspired a song called 'Mein Teil' by provocative German techno-rockers Rammstein.

A photograph of Christina Long held up by Shelley Riling, her aunt, on the day of Sol Dos Reis's sentencing in September 2003.

Inset: Saul Dos Reis is taken down on the day he was convicted of killing a teenage girl he met on the Internet. He was already serving 30 years for killing Long.

Top: Music teacher Jane Longhurst, who was killed by Graham Coutts in March 2003.

Bottom: CCTV footage from the Big Yellow Box Storage Company in Brighton, showing Graham Coutts removing a cardboard box containing Jane Longhurst's body.

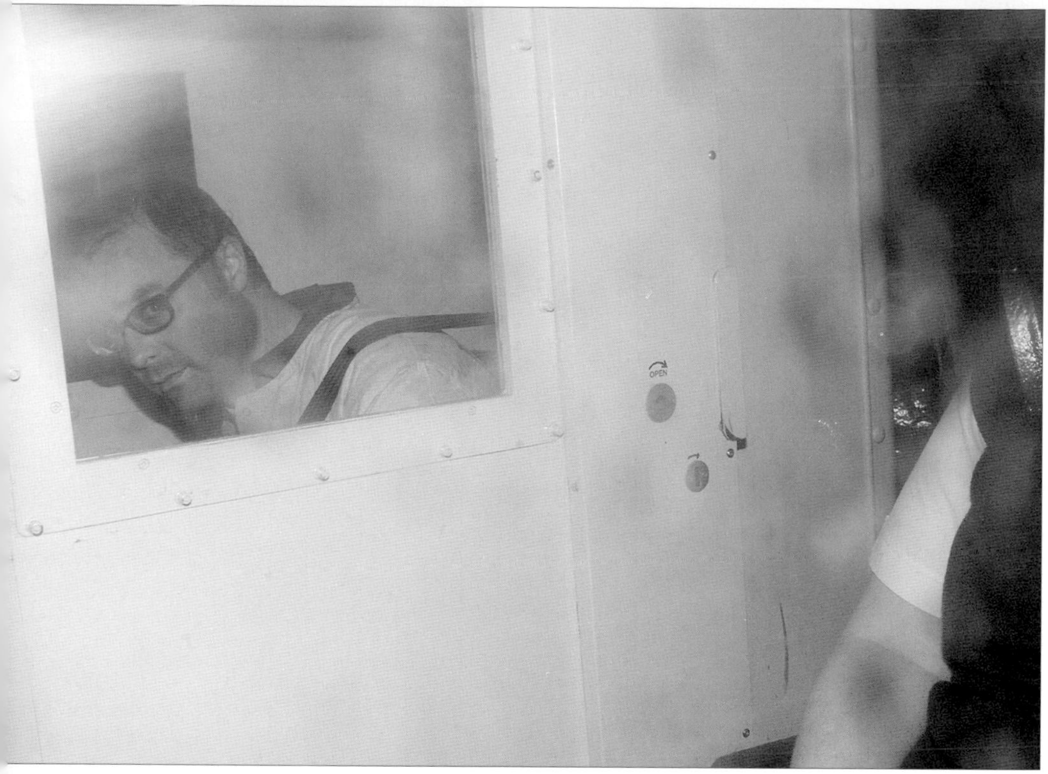

Top: Coutts was transported by special police van from Lewes court wearing a yellow jumpsuit emblazoned with 'Category A', denoting the most dangerous kind of criminal. He sat in a secure box within the van watched by an officer, as shown in this rare shot captured by a photographer waiting outside the court.

Left: Graham Coutts, before his conviction for the murder of Jane Longhurst.

Top: Darlie Routier in court, charged with the murder of her two sons.

Bottom: Bodies-in-barrels killer John E Robinson faces the court in January 2002.

Both Devon (*top*) and Damon (*bottom*) Routier were murdered in their home in Rowlett, Texas, in June 1996. *AP Photo/The Dallas Morning News/Empics*

Nancy Ann Kissel leaves court shortly after pleading not guilty to murdering her husband in Hong Kong.

the evidence to implicate someone they decided must have done it? A growing chorus of internet observers believes so. A juror from the trial now says that he and his fellow jurors made the wrong decision. The author of one of the true-crime books has also changed her mind, claiming that the jury heard perjured testimony and were never shown photos that would have proved Darlie was a victim of a savage attack. Adding fuel to the fire, her defenders claim to have found over 30,000 inconsistencies and errors in the court stenographer's trial transcript.

Even the most experienced legal eagles have found themselves sucked in by the Routier saga. In March 2004, in oral arguments before the Texas Court of Criminal Appeals into whether procedural flaws were made during the original trial, the nine judges began peppering lawyers with questions on other aspects of the case.

Was there, they asked, an insurance policy on the children, which might have given Darlie a reason to kill them?

When Darlie talked to homicide detectives, did she make any kind of confession?

But the most baffling question about the murders has yet to be answered: why would someone show up in a nice new suburban neighbourhood, target a house on a well-lit cul-de-sac, enter through a garage screen window a few feet from a dog's basket, navigate his way through a darkened utility room, grab a butcher knife from the kitchenette and then head into the living room to stab two boys and slash their mother's throat? Robbery was almost immediately ruled out as a motive; nor, police determined, did anyone have a grudge against the family.

The Texas Department of Corrections website makes the facts of the case simple and concise:

> 'Darlie Lynn Routier, inmate number 999220, currently sits on Death Row, Texas, convicted of the brutal stabbing deaths of her five-year-old son, Damon, and his six-year-old brother, Devon. On Thursday, 6 June 1996, they were murdered as they slept in a downstairs room with their mother at their family home in Rowlett.
>
> 'Routier's husband, Darin, and infant son, Drake, slept through the attack in upstairs bedrooms and they were not harmed. Darlie Routier, who claimed that she was also asleep at the time also suffered stab wounds during the attack but police say that they were self-inflicted. In her defence, she claimed to have awakened to see a black man fleeing the residence.
>
> 'Prosecutors argued that she killed her sons because they interfered with the lifestyle she wanted to live. She was arrested after making two inconsistent statements to the police.'

In the early hours of Thursday, 6 June 1996, a 911 emergency telephone call was put through to the Rowlett Police Department at 4401 Rowlett Road, Dallas County, Texas. The midnight dispatcher, Doris Trammell, took the call and identified the caller's address as 5801 Eagle Drive.

The first police officer to arrive at the scene was David Waddell, who was soon joined by Sergeant Matthew Walling. Paramedics Jack Kolbye and Brian Koschak rushed through the front door to find Devon dead; he had been stabbed twice in the chest with such force that the knife had passed almost all the way through his body.

Damon was still clinging on to life; he had been stabbed half a dozen or more times in the back.

Darlie, who had also been sleeping downstairs with her sons, had knife wounds in her right forearm and her left shoulder and her throat had been cut. Doctors said she survived only because the knife stopped two millimetres short of her carotid artery. No one, either at the house or later in the hospital's emergency trauma room, noticed any bruises on her wrists and arms.

Other medics soon turned up. Larry Byford, Eric Zimmerman and Rick Coleman assisted where they could and Damon was rushed to the Baylor Medical Center, where he was certified dead on arrival.

CID Commander Lieutenant Grant Jack had been on the force for 20 years. He was summoned from his bed and at 3am arrived at the murder scene, where he met Detective Jimmy Patterson, a veteran of the Crimes Against Persons Division. Patterson explained to his superior what little he knew about the incident: that the mother claimed a stranger had committed the atrocities and a bloodstained butcher knife – the murder weapon – lay on the worktop in the utility room.

Lieutenant Jack put Patterson and his partner, Chris Frosch, in charge of the investigation and Frosch sped off to the hospital to interview Darlie Routier at the first opportunity. He needed to get as much detailed information as he could about what had happened to cause such blood-letting and havoc.

In a written statement given to the police a few days later, Darlie, then 26, told the following story.

She was awakened by Damon's cries of 'Mommy! Mommy!' In the dark, she said, she didn't even notice she had been stabbed several times and that her carotid artery had almost been severed. She did, however, see a man moving through the kitchen and she followed him as he went towards the garage. When she got to the utility room, she saw a knife and picked it up. Only then, she said, did she return to find Devon and Damon and realise that she had been stabbed too. Darin, who was sleeping upstairs with their infant son Drake, came downstairs after hearing his wife's screams and began administering cardiopulmonary resuscitation to Devon. By then the assailant had disappeared.

A few days later, Darlie Routier would significantly change this account.

Blonde, hazel-eyed Darlie was born in Altoona, Pennsylvania, on 4 January 1970. As a teenager she was attractive to boys, among them Darin Routier. Darin worked in a Western Sizzler restaurant alongside Darlie's mother, who found him a bright, talkative good-looking boy with ambitious plans for his future. He would be, she figured, a good catch for her oldest daughter. Playing matchmaker, she introduced the two kids and by all reports it was love at first sight for both of them.

The dark-haired tall boy with wavy hair flipped for the five-foot-three, heart-faced Lubbock, Texas, belle with the big eyes. And she, in turn, for him.

The couple dated in high school and continued to correspond after Darin, two years older than Darlie, went away to a technical college in Dallas. However, at Darin's going-away party Darlie showed a possessive and cunning nature that had lain hidden beneath her surface sweetness. She became annoyed that she wasn't getting enough attention, so she left the party. Then she came back frantic, claiming that someone had tried to rape her.

'That ruse gave her just the attention that she craved,' said a friend, and this incident was a portent of things to come.

After graduating from high school, Darlie joined Darin in Dallas, where he had been hired as a technician at a computer chip company. Darlie landed a job with the same firm and they lived together while saving their money until, in August 1988, they married. The couple honeymooned first-class in Jamaica.

On returning to Texas, the newlyweds first moved into an apartment in Garland, close to where Darin worked learning the booming computer chip industry. Within a year, they relocated to a home in conservative Rowlett, a small town as neat as a pin. Here Darin started a home-based company named Testnec which tested circuit boards for computers.

Their first child was born in 1989 – a healthy boy named Devon Rush – to be followed by another son in 1991 – Damon Christian. With two children and a fast-growing business, the Routiers found it necessary to rent space in an office building. Their life seemed to be fulfilling the American Dream.

By 1992, their company had earned them a small fortune. The up-and-coming couple yearned to enjoy the prestige they felt was due to them and had a house built in Dalrock Heights Addition, an affluent suburb of Rowlett, some eight miles north-east of Dallas and adjacent to shimmering Lake Ray Hubbard. This was a model community of upper-class business people, crime-free streets and happy families who drove Subaru pickups in which they would convey their kids half a block to school.

The $130,000 two-storey home of neo-Georgian design was a miniature mansion replete with classic porch, colonial shutters and a working fountain on the front lawn. Complementing their new life, the family boasted a Jaguar that sat gleaming on a circular driveway.

By all accounts, Darlie was happy. She was a very good mother, doting on her two children, living to celebrate the good times with them. At Christmas, their house was the most illuminated in the area. At Halloween, their windows displayed more goblins than any other. At Thanksgiving, it was said, the Routiers' turkey was the largest and tastiest. On the children's birthdays, Darlie threw gorgeous parties inviting classmates for an afternoon of frolics in their spacious entertainment centre.

There was never any suggestion that Mrs Routier did not love her children, and, for his part, Darin wore shirts with the sleeves rolled up to show his muscles, grew his hair long at the back, and sported a diamond watch and several gold-nugget-and-diamond rings. He doted on his kids, too.

But there was another side to Darlie, claim some who knew her – a side that loved to show off to cover a low self-esteem. She revelled in materialism and creating an impression, often to the point of the bizarre.

She had 36-DDD breast implants that she further accentuated by wearing tight-fitting tops, she made regular visits to the tanning salon and wore diamond rings on every finger, she bought a toy Pomeranian with white hair matching her own. When she bought clothes, they were revealing outfits she wore for a night's dancing just to grab the attention of onlookers, and her wardrobe bills skyrocketed.

Darlie's detractors – there are always plenty of those with jealousies and axes to grind – say that her need to be the flashiest, gaudiest woman around eventually overcame everything else in her life – including her children. Neighbours complained that Damon and Devon, not far past the toddler stage, were left unsupervised. And, when Darlie did attend to them, she often seemed frustrated at having to take the time to do so. Her patience with them, it was said, had waned.

The roots of domestic problems surfaced when guests at a Christmas party silently watched as Darlie and Darin argued violently when she danced too many times with another man, fuelling rumours of extramarital dating by both partners. But the couple continued to play the surface charade, buying, buying and buying.

Then they splashed out on a 27-foot cabin cruiser and a space for it at the exclusive Lake Ray Hubbard Marina.

In 1995, research shows, Darin's company brought in about half a million dollars in gross revenues, from which he paid himself a salary of $125,000. 'At the time, we were in the top 2 per cent of the tax bracket for our age,' he boasted. And they spent every cent they made, with almost $12,000 worth of new equipment being purchased for the flourishing business. However, the flip side of the coin is that the Routiers' tax return for that year indicated a gross income of $264,000 and, with a profit margin of 40 per cent, the couple netted a little over $100,000.

But, if the financial problems were causing stress in their marriage, no one in the neighbourhood saw it. Their neighbours thought they were a hoot, Rowlett's version of the Clampetts from *The Beverly Hillbillies*. Then Darin got behind on the bills; he was at least a month late on the mortgage and owed $10,000 in back taxes to the IRS and $12,000 on credit cards.

With his finances in serious trouble, Darin decided to start a second business, which he called Champagne Wishes. He would take people around the lake on his boat at sunset while they sipped Champagne and, if they wished, avail themselves of the vessel's sleeping quarters.

However, Darin's difficulties didn't seem to concern Darlie: her shopping didn't slow down and she made plans to take a trip that summer to Cancun, Mexico, with some girlfriends.

Nevertheless, even if they were a little flashy, the Routiers were not disliked. One neighbour called them 'the Ozzie and Harriet of the nineties'. Darlie was known as a cookie-baking housewife who always let the local kids hang out at her home, which they called 'the Nintendo House' because of the elaborate games room that Darin had designed. She cooked for neighbours going through hard times and generously made a mortgage payment for a neighbour with cancer.

Friends who were aware of the Routiers' problems were happy when Darlie became pregnant early in 1995; they counted on the new baby as the catalyst to renew the couple's love for each other. But, after Drake was born in October that year, Darlie suffered post-natal depression. Mood swings brought on sudden tempers and dark rages. She piled on weight.

Not helping matters was the state of the couple's finances, which, despite good business profits from Testnec, did not meet the exorbitant lifestyle they preferred to live and had grown used to.

Suddenly ends did not meet.

Darlie was unable to shed the weight she had acquired since her pregnancy and grew increasingly antagonistic. She took diet pills that didn't work – a fact that Darin would remind her of when the couple battled, knowing it was her tender spot.

Darlie sporadically kept a diary. There were times she would attend to it daily, followed by long absences. On Friday, 3 May 1996, and contemplating suicide, she wrote, 'Devon, Damon and Drake, I hope you will forgive me for what I am about to do. My life has been such a hard fight for a long time, and I just can't find the strength to keep fighting any more. I love you three more than anything else in this world and I want all three of you to be healthy and happy and I don't want you to see a miserable person every time you look at me...'

On that day, she considered taking some sleeping pills to kill herself. But she never swallowed them and didn't finish her diary entry either. After talking with her on the phone, Darin became worried and drove home to comfort her. She told him she was ashamed of what she had done and would never think about taking her life again. Darlie said her 'blah feeling', as she put it, was because she hadn't had a period in more than a year. When it arrived a few days after her suicidal thoughts, she said, her spirits soared. In fact, people who saw her in the weeks that followed say she did not seem particularly despondent.

Her old friend Barbara Jovell did tell Darlie that she should get some counselling or perhaps enter a treatment centre, as she herself had done when she once felt suicidal, but Jovell didn't sense that Darlie was desperate or self-destructive.

In late May, Darlie and Darin took the boys to Scarborough Faire, a festival featuring characters dressed in medieval costumes. Darlie, flamboyant as always, wore a silky belly-dancing outfit. Nevertheless, any cost-cutting measures were still ignored and spending sprees accelerated, so that their financial troubles deepened. Testnec was haemorrhaging money and

Darin was unable to pay himself the salary he required, nor pay Darlie anything at all for doing the books, which she had let go in her depression.

Creditors were now circling like vultures and demanded payment of late bills, and crunch time came on 1 June 1996, when the Routiers' bank flatly denied them a much-needed loan of $5,000. The ship was sinking; the refusal of a financial lifeboat was the beginning of the end.

Later, at Darlie's trial, Okie Williams of Bank One said the loan application by Darin was initially denied on 1 June. He said the request was rejected a second time, on 3 June, 'because of excessive obligations in relation to income, and related reasons'.

On Wednesday, 5 June, the boys played in the hot tub, and that evening Damon and Devon huddled under blankets in front of a television Darin had just installed in the living room. Darlie and Darin would later say they stayed up talking past midnight, then kissed each other goodnight. Darin went upstairs to the master bedroom, where seven-month-old Drake was asleep in his cot, while Darlie curled up on the couch downstairs next to the two older boys. She had been sleeping on the couch that week, she said, because she wanted to watch over Damon and Devon, who had been spending the night downstairs since school had finished, and because she was a light sleeper and would sometimes be awakened by Drake turning over in his cot.

A few hours later, the 911 dispatcher in Rowlett received a frantic call. 'Somebody came in here,' Darlie screamed down the phone. 'They just stabbed me and my children!'

Having examined from a distance the larger, although incomplete, picture, we can now move in closer and start to study several of its components. First, the fingerprints, which, according to the pro-Darlie camp and her legal team, are an integral part of proving her innocence. For among the few fly-specking issues that her supporters have seized on is the fingerprint evidence – or, to be correct, the lack of fingerprint evidence – which they believe may prove her innocence.

Darlie had told the police dispatcher that a man wielding a knife had attacked her and her sons. She said the assailant had dropped the knife when he fled the house and that she picked it up. The dispatcher told her not to touch anything, to which Darlie responded with a calculated comment, totally out of sync with the rest of the call: 'God… I bet if we could have gotten the prints maybe… maybe…'

This being the case, there would have been no fingerprints on the knife other than those of Darlie Routier, who obviously wanted it on record that she had picked up the murder weapon – thus any prints found on it she had 'inadvertently' placed there, conveniently erasing the alleged attacker's at the same time.

Crime-scene technicians had discovered a hazy fingerprint on a coffee table in the recreation room. The table was very close to where Damon had been stabbed. At the trial, prosecution experts argued that it was a child's print, while the defence team claimed it was an adult's.

By a process of elimination, it was determined that the print apparently had not been left by Darlie, Darin or any of the investigators or emergency personnel who attended the scene of the murders. The police did not fingerprint the dead children at the time, and since the children were soon buried their prints could not be compared with the print on the coffee table.

Devon and Damon's bodies were exhumed several years ago and a post-mortem photograph was taken of the print from Devon's right thumb. Family members also found a set of Damon's fingerprints which had been taken as part of a school safety programme.

Fingerprint consultant and former police detective Robert C Lohnes Sr said the coffee table print ruled out Darin, Darlie and Devon, leaving only Damon's prints to be matched. On this matter, lead prosecutor Greg Davis says Darlie Routier 'has since been unusually quiet'!

At the time of the case, Greg Davis believed the coffee table fingerprint could have been Damon's. Other blood trace evidence supported this theory because, unlike Devon, who was stabbed through the heart and never moved, Damon was very close to the table and he had moved after the attack.

Greg Davis has more recently stated, 'If there was a fingerprint discrepancy, the prints could have been matched up at the time [they found the school card]. The family could have seen whether the fingerprint matched Damon's. They [Darlie Routier and her internet supporters] haven't talked about that at all.'

The organisers of the internet's Free Darlie Routier Campaign have also relied heavily on a latent fingerprint expert called Richard L Jantz, and in doing so they may have inadvertently shot themselves in the foot.

Rather than using more accepted fingerprinting investigation techniques, Jantz used methods more commonly employed by anthropologists in his efforts to size, age and determine the sex of the person who left the coffee table print. This technique, however, has brought some quite unwarranted criticism from the anti-Routier camp and the state's attorney. Nevertheless, although Jantz was quite sure that it was a child's print, he clearly stated that, although the print *did not appear* to match prints from Darlie, 'it does not rule out the Appellant [Darlie Routier] nor does it rule out any partner, adult male or adult female'.

In summary, the print on the coffee table could have originated from any adult male or female, or even young Damon. If it had been proven not to have been left by the dead boy, then no doubt Darlie Routier would be advertising the fact at every opportunity, but prosecutor Davis says she is not, so I will leave readers to form their own conclusions on this point.

Two other unidentifiable fingerprints were found on the utility room door through which Darlie Routier says the murderer fled. It is now claimed by her internet supporters that further examination of these two fingerprints is critical to her claim that an unknown man attacked her.

The first and most important print lifted from this door was a latent bloody fingerprint – whoever left it had blood on their finger. Nevertheless, it revealed insufficient detail to identify its source, although forensic fingerprint analyst Glenn Langenburg has currently excluded its having come from Darlie Routier, while other experts argue that it cannot exclude her.

The second print taken from the door was a latent print located below the patent bloody fingerprint. On behalf of ABC News, latent print consultant Robert Lohnes analysed this print in June 2003 and pro-Routier supporters conclude that it matched Darin Routier's second finger joint on the middle finger of the left hand. At least this is what Darlie's legal team claimed in their 'Renewed Motion for Testing of Physical and Biological Evidence and Request for an Evidentiary Hearing', which was granted by the Honourable Robert Francis.

The documents are posted on the website dedicated to Routier's release and on closer scrutiny I suggest that the court papers have been released primarily to blow smoke in a critic's eyes.

I can support this cutting observation because fingerprint consultant Robert Lohnes said nothing of the kind. In his Affidavit, sworn on 29 January 2003, Lohnes mentions nothing about Darin Routier's fingerprints. Quite the contrary, in fact, because he simply says that, after comparing a photograph of the bloodied print with the fingerprint card of Darlie Routier, he was able to confirm that the prints did not come from her.

Glenn Langenburg also analysed the second latent print from the door. From the prints available to him for comparison – which included the fingerprints, finger joints and upper palm areas for Darlie and Darin Routier – Langenburg was unable to match the latent fingerprint to either person. Significantly, he was unable to say that Darlie Routier had not left this print.

However, if Darin had left this second print, the significance is worthless, for he lived in the house and his dabs would be everywhere.

Quite obviously, the value of the unidentifiable latent fingerprints found at the crime scene will be of little value in Darlie Routier's struggle to have her sentence quashed. If, however, any of the three prints had been clear enough, possibly they could have been added to a fingerprint database which would automatically have scanned its registers for a match – perhaps flagging up a known offender with a previous criminal record. If this had been successful, Routier might have solid grounds for an appeal because it would have been proved that an intruder had been in the home that fateful night.

Shedding of blood is the dramatic accompaniment to murder committed by violent means. Blood accounts for about 9 per cent of a healthy person's body weight and, as many murderers have discovered to their cost, when it is spilled, a little goes a long way.

While crime-scene technicians methodically worked their way through the Routiers' home, in the utility room/kitchenette Sergeant Nabors noted that, while the sink was spotless and white, the top and edges of the surfaces around and above it were blood-smudged. It was as if someone had taken the effort to clean the sink of blood and wipe the worktops.

Initially, Darlie denied ever being at the sink, although when later pressed she changed her story. Of more significance, however, is the fact that she made no mention of her washing her hands, or the intruder stopping to wash his hands in the sink as he fled the premises – an action that in any event would have been unlikely.

With this in mind, Nabors conducted a Luminol test to detect the presence of human blood that cannot be seen with the naked eye. If the white crystalline compound in the Luminol detected the copper component found in human blood, the area sprayed would become luminescent. The sergeant sprayed the sink and the surrounding counter. When the lights were switched off, the entire sink basin and the surrounding surface glowed a brilliant bluish light in the dark. He concluded that the bloodstains discovered in the sink would be consistent with someone washing blood off his or her hands. And there was also an indication that some of the blood around the sink had been wiped up with a towel. Hardly the actions of a crazed killer intent on escaping as fast as he could!

Although Darlie Routier vehemently denied visiting the sink to wash her wounds, the only scenario one can infer from the blood traces in the sink and on the worktop was that she had cut her own throat at the sink and then tried to wipe up the blood afterwards. But there is significantly more to this than meets the eye.

If she did wash her hands in the sink, when did she do it, and why clean the sink and wipe the worktop? These actions could have only taken place *after* murdering her sons, stabbing herself and cutting her own throat, and *before* picking up the phone to dial 911, because she stayed on the phone until assistance arrived, and by then the sink had already been cleaned.

This being the only conclusion that can be reached, it would also be reasonable to ask, what else did she do during the period between the murders and calling for help?

Perhaps of even more significance was the fact that only Darlie's bloodied footprints were visible on the floor. Surely, if the killer had stopped to wash his hands, with blood dripping on to the floor, his own shoeprints would have been found, but they were not.

Fragments of a shattered wine glass lay on and around Darlie's bloody footprints. A vacuum cleaner lay on its side. Blood found *underneath* these items indicated to crime-scene consultant James Cron that they were dropped after – not before or during – the violence and the spilling of blood.

Sergeant Nabors repeated the Luminol process on the leatherette couch close to where the boys had been stabbed. Here he found a small child's handprint glowing iridescent blue on the edge of the couch. Like the blood in the kitchen sink, someone had wiped the blood away. The police had not wiped the couch clean, so who had? Surely not the alleged intruder?

The only two people who could have wiped it were Darlie and her husband, and they denied doing so.

In summary, the sink had been cleaned, the blood-smeared worktop wiped over, a bloodstain on the couch had been wiped too, and all before the police arrived at the premises. Despite all this, the Routiers denied cleaning anything.

To evaluate the veracity of Darlie's statements to the police, a forensics expert tried to replicate the intruder's series of moves that fateful night, based on Darlie's recollection.

He began by dropping a bloody knife from waist height on to the floor of the utility room while making his way towards the garage door. The blood that spattered across the floor during the test produced a pattern entirely different from the little pools found in the utility room on the night of the murders. The test conducted by the forensics expert showed a random pattern of drops and directional splashes, while the crime photos showed 'carefully dropped drips of blood'.

When another blood expert found tiny drops of the boys' blood on the back of the nightshirt that Darlie had worn that evening, he remarked that a likely way the blood could have got there was when it dripped off the butcher knife and on to Darlie's back, and this would be consistent with her raising her arm above her while stabbing the boys.

After the murders, Darlie gave two conflicting accounts of exactly what the intruder had done to her. One officer said that she told him that she had struggled with her assailant on the couch, while another officer said she told him the struggle was at the work surface of the utility room.

To retrace the alleged attacker's movements as observed by Darlie Routier, James Cron then followed the trail of blood. It indeed led from the room where the children had been slain, through to a utility room, past the sink, then on to the concrete floor of the garage, where it trailed off below a window screen. Cron then went out into the yard and began looking for blood traces that might have been left behind by the alleged slayer in flight after he exited the garage window. Surely his savagery would have produced vast amounts of blood and his clothing would have been dripping with it – yet there was no blood on the window, its frame or sill, or on the outer wall.

There was no blood in the dewy, wet mulch below the window... or on the yard's manicured lawn... or along or on top of the six-foot-high fence that surrounded the garden, or on the gate, or in the nearby alley.

The blood was contained within the house, and nowhere else!

Darlie Routier had told the police that she had seen the killer leave the premises by passing through the utility room and into the garage before disappearing. The blood trail led to the window screen and not to the garage doors, which, as Darin claimed in court, were in any case locked.

The screen had been slashed with a knife, but on examination it showed no signs of having been forcibly pushed in or out to facilitate an adult's ingress or egress. Even more telling was the fact that the screen's frame was easily removable. Perhaps, the investigators figured, the woman, in her panicked condition, may have been wrong – perhaps the intruder had found another means of entry and exit. So they examined every entry point to the entire home for other indications of breaking and entering.

They looked for other blood trails and found nothing. Why, the police asked themselves, didn't the intruder just pull off the screen, as burglars normally do?

Then Charles Linch, Dallas County's premier trace-evidence analyst, dropped a bombshell: he found a bread knife in the kitchen drawer. On the serrated blade he discovered a nearly invisible fibre, 60 microns long, made of fibreglass coated with rubber. Using a microscope, Linch determined that the fibre found on the bread knife matched in every respect the composition of the fibreglass in the mesh screen cut by the so-called intruder. If this was the knife used to cut the screen, and there is no doubt that it was, common sense tells us that the screen was cut from inside the house, not by the intruder from the outside.

This is not *Star Trek*. The intruder was not beamed into the house, where he searched for a bread knife, then beamed back outside to cut the screen, to climb through, replace the bread knife, kill the boys, attack the mother and flee. No! Only someone already inside the house, someone who knew where a suitable knife was – one of the parents – could have cut the screen and placed the knife back in the drawer.

The police considered every single other option, but still the window screen seemed an unlikely escape route even though Darlie was insistent that this was the way the killer left the house.

If an intruder had entered and escaped through this slash in the screen, he would have left some trace of his doing so – perhaps a human hair, a fibre from his clothing or a blood trace – but nothing was found. The dust on the sill was undisturbed, there were no handprints, bloody or otherwise around the window; odd, since the killer, in forcing his way through the window, would have had to hang on to the walls for balance, and yet not a boot- or shoeprint was found in the soft mulch outside!

All of this led the police to conclude that the trail of blood leading to the window screen was a red herring. Someone was trying to deceive them into believing that the killer was an intruder when no intruder had ever existed. But who would try to deceive them? If the intruder did not exist, and there is not a shred of evidence – apart from Darlie Routier's statement – that there was one, Darlie Routier was lying. By 'arranging' the crime scene and scattering red herrings around, she was trying to divert suspicion away from herself.

In the entertainment room where, according to Darlie, she struggled with her attacker, James Cron found little evidence of a melee having taken place. The lampshade was askew and an expensive flower arrangement lay beside the coffee table. There was nothing more out of place. He found, in fact, the fragile stems of the flowers unbroken – as if the arrangement hadn't fallen but been placed there. Once again, someone was trying to deceive the eye. But there was even more.

Atop the utility room work surface, close to the sink, sat Darlie's purse, which appeared in order and undisturbed. Several pieces of jewellery – rings, a bracelet and a watch – were laid out neatly and untouched. If the alleged intruder's motive had been robbery, he would have seen the jewellery when he washed his hands and stolen it. Therefore, it was obvious that, before cutting her own throat and injuring herself, Darlie had removed her jewellery to protect it from blood contamination or possible damage. It was a repeat of the staged scene in the murder room: items had been carefully placed to avoid damaging them, and even a bloodstain on the couch had been wiped away.

Darlie Routier had inflicted her own injuries at the sink!

Everything the crime-scene experts saw at the crime scene disturbed them. The lack of a blood trail away from the home, coupled with virtually no signs of a struggle, bothered them most. The entire picture before them had been carefully set. Everything had been designed, like one of Escher's drawings, to fool the eye into seeing something that did not exist.

Of great significance is that Darlie must have injured herself, arranged the crime scene and set the red herrings *after* the murders had been committed and *before* the 911 call was made. The actions of a very cold and calculated killer indeed!

After his thorough and all-day examination of the crime scene, James Cron summarised his findings for Lieutenant Jack and Sergeant Walling: 'We all know the crime scene tells the story. Problem is, that story's not the same one the mother's telling. Somebody inside this house did this thing. Gentlemen, there was no intruder.'

Cron was positive that the crime scene had been staged. An article in the FBI's *Law Enforcement Bulletin* refers to 'staging':

> 'Offenders who stage crime scenes usually make mistakes because they arrange the scene to resemble what they believe it should look like. In so doing, offenders experience a great deal of stress and do not have the time to fit all the pieces together logically. As a result, inconsistencies in forensic findings and in the overall "big picture" of the crime scene will begin to appear. These inconsistencies can serve as the "red flags" of staging, which serve to prevent investigations from becoming misguided.'

But nobody asked: 'Why hadn't the Routiers' dog barked in the night?'

As Sherlock Holmes would be quick to deduce, the dog knew the killer/s and that could have only been Darlie Routier, Darin Routier or both.

With the physical evidential facts already established, all of which prove beyond any doubt that no intruder had entered the Routiers' home on the night of the murders and that the crime scene had been 'carefully staged' by someone living in the house, we can now focus more closely on the crimes in an effort to prove that only Darlie Routier, acting alone, could have committed the murders.

Darlie Routier most certainly had the opportunity for committing the crime and she had the opportunity to prepare for the crime, clean the place up and scatter red herrings around to divert suspicion away from herself.

The scientific forensic testimony had proven, beyond any doubt, that an intruder did not leave the blood trail. The fibre found on the bread knife taken from the drawer and replaced in the drawer matched in every respect fibres from the mesh window screen, and this evidence convinced the jury that a guilty verdict was safe.

The police were convinced that the killer had tampered with and fabricated evidence at the crime scene in an effort to lead them in the wrong direction – to point an accusatory finger elsewhere. This being so, it was an act by the killer indicative of guilty consciousness or intent. And Darlie Routier certainly gave a number of unsatisfactory explanations as to the events that night.

At first, she told one officer she had struggled with her assailant on the couch. She added that her only view of the man came as he was walking away from the couch. She said she just couldn't remember any distinct details about the attack or the killer, except that he was wearing dark clothes and a baseball cap.

To support this claim, she also told a friend, who visited her in hospital, that she remembered lying on the couch as the man was running the knife over her face. When she returned home from hospital, an annoyed Darlie told a shocked friend that the place was a mess and would take some cleaning up.

However, when questioned about the blood in the sink, and over the work surfaces, she told another officer a different story: that the struggle took place at the sink.

The investigators' suspicions grew even more when the doctors and nurses who treated Darlie told them that her wounds could have been self-inflicted. Then, a few days after leaving the hospital, she showed the police bruises that covered her arms from wrist to elbow. These, she said, had been caused by her attacker. Yet the doctors who examined her said the bruises were too fresh to have been inflicted on the night of the murders. More likely, they said, Darlie hit her arms with a blunt instrument after she left the hospital – or got someone else to do it – to convince the police that she had been attacked.

The police asked themselves: why did the alleged intruder only slice Darlie's throat and stab her in the shoulder and forearm, instead of plunging his knife deep into her body, the way he plunged it into the bodies of her boys? Why did he not make sure that Darlie was dead so that she would be unable to identify him or raise the alarm?

If there had been an intruder, what was his motive? It most

certainly was not robbery. But Darlie Routier's motive for committing the crime has not been found.

Or has it?

One of the first police officers at the scene was perplexed because Darlie didn't tend to her sons, even when he asked her to. Instead, she held a towel to her own neck. A slash of the butcher knife had missed her carotid artery by two millimetres, or was it a carefully judged act of self-mutilation? As no intruder had attacked her, only Darlie could have injured herself. We can rule out her husband because his wife's injuries spilled a large amount of blood and there was not a drop of blood on him when the police arrived – unless he had changed his clothes.

Nurses at the hospital to which Darlie was taken said that when she was told that her sons were dead she exhibited a 'flat affect' and did not dissolve into hysteria, as mothers often do on learning they have lost a child.

When Darlie took the stand at her trial, she changed her story, explaining that she went to the sink to wet towels and place them on her children's wounds. Paramedics found no towels near the children when they arrived, but Darlie was holding a towel to her own neck.

She also claimed that the scene with the Silly String at Devon's grave was her heartfelt way of wishing a happy birthday to her son, who, she hoped, was watching from heaven. But Darlie was not a persuasive witness. She cried at unlikely times and became far too defensive under the cross-examination of Toby Shook, the veteran Dallas County prosecutor, who kept slamming her for what he called her 'selective amnesia'.

The facts proved that there had been no murderous intruder in the Routiers' home, so Darlie had been lying. She had even laid false clues and tampered with evidence. This, combined with giving unsatisfactory explanations and changing her account of what took place, tied in with her detached post-crime behaviour, and earned her a place on Death Row.

But there was just one problem.

On the night of the murders, one of Darin's socks was found down a back alley some 75 yards away from the house. It contained two small spots of blood from Damon and Devon, but none of Darlie's blood.

What was it doing there?

The police initially speculated that Darlie had carried the sock three houses away to make it look as if the intruder had dropped it during his escape. But they couldn't find any of Darlie's blood – or anyone else's blood – outside the house. There was no blood on the back patio, on the back fence or in the back alley. If Darlie had planted the sock, how did she avoid leaving a blood trail of her own for, once her throat was cut, she lost significant amounts of blood.

The detectives and the prosecutors came up with an interesting theory: Darlie stabbed her boys to death, took the sock down the alley – perhaps to give the impression that the intruder had used it to keep his prints off the knife – then cut herself at the kitchen sink.

Either before she stabbed the boys, or before she stabbed herself, she cut the mesh screen with the bread knife, laid the red herrings, arranged the crime scene and, once all that was done, called 911, then screamed out for Darin.

However, Darlie's well-meaning internet supporters argue, if she had wanted the police to find the sock, wouldn't she have thrown it closer to the house, perhaps at the end of the driveway, instead of leaving it so far away, next to a garbage can, where the police might have overlooked it? And wouldn't she have doused that sock in blood so that the police would know what they had found? And even then, would Darlie have had time to do everything before the police arrived?

In fact, had there been an intruder who used the sock to avoid leaving his fingerprints, he would have left his dabs at the point of entry – but none was there. The stabbings were brutal and blood would have sprayed all over the sock, and on exiting the premises the blood-soaked sock would have smeared the window and its frame, as well as any door frame it may have touched. But there were only a few spots of blood on the sock. To suggest that an intruder slipped it on his hand before he killed the boys is ludicrous.

There was no intruder, so the only people who could have dropped the sock were Darlie and Darin. But there is no evidence to implicate Darin in the murders or any attempt to cover them up, so we must focus on Darlie. We have seen that she certainly spent some time arranging things and cleaning up before the police turned up, so I suggest that this is another of Darlie's red herrings in her efforts to divert suspicion from herself. However, when the red herrings fail, the opposite occurs and she puts her head firmly in the noose.

The pro-Routier camp have been thorough, in one respect, by highlighting the police records which indicate that Darlie was on the phone with the 911 dispatcher for five minutes and 44 seconds. Just as that call was ending, a police officer came into the house and he was there for at least a minute before the paramedics arrived. They found Damon still breathing; he died shortly thereafter. Why is that important? Darlie's supporters ask.

According to a doctor who studied the severity and location of Damon's stab wounds, the boy could not have lived longer than nine minutes once he was first stabbed and probably lived no more than six minutes after that.

'Let's assume he lived nine minutes,' claim Darlie Routier and her friends. 'If you subtract from that nine minutes her five-minute-and-44-second phone call to 911, then subtract the additional minute and ten seconds that she was in the presence of a police officer, Darlie had only two minutes and six seconds to stab her sons, head for the garage, step through the slit in the window screen, jump a back fence or go through a back gate, run barefoot for 75 yards down an alley, drop a bloody sock, run 75 yards back, stab herself, clean up the blood around the sink, and stage whatever crime scene there was left to be staged.'

The prosecutors certainly did not have a good answer to the timeline conundrum, except to say that the doctor was simply guessing about the nine minutes it took Damon to die and that even then Darlie could have had enough time to commit the murders and stage the crime scene.

Leaping on the prosecutor's uncertainty, the pro-Routier camp asks, 'But, if she was smart enough to plant fake evidence, wouldn't she have been ready with a more believable story about what the intruder looked like, and how the killings occurred?'

But it is the sock we are interested in, and not the what-ifs.

The sock did belong to Damon. Forensic experts did find spots of both of the dead boys' blood on it, and that blood could have only got there after the murders had been committed, therefore, before the mother injured herself.

With the alleged intruder now ruled out, the sock could have only been placed where it was found by one of the parents, so the pro-Routier followers have missed the point entirely.

In assuming that the suggested timeline proves her innocence, Darlie Routier shoots herself in both feet, because it was proved that only someone who lived in the house could have used the bread knife to slash the mesh screen, and that screen was not entered or exited by anyone. No one had stepped into the dew-wet mulch outside the window, rushed across the lawn, jumped a back fence or went through the back gate. So we can safely remove from the equation the time it would have taken to accomplish this alleged sequence of actions.

In fact, Darlie Routier simply opened her front door, dashed to where she dropped the sock and returned to the house, where she cut her throat, cleaned up the blood in the kitchen and called 911.

What really makes no sense was why their mother would choose to kill Damon and Devon at all. If, as the police and the prosecutors believed, Darlie had become increasingly upset about money, why didn't she murder Darin and cash in his $800,000 life insurance policy? The policies on Damon and Devon totalled only $10,000, and their funerals alone cost more than $14,000. If she was overwhelmed by the stresses of motherhood – another theory – then why didn't she also kill Drake, the baby, who required most of her attention?

Of course, Drake was in bed next to his father.

At her trial, Darlie's lawyer, Doug Mulder, one of Dallas's most prominent and charismatic criminal defence attorneys, kept asking the jurors if they really believed that a doting mother could, in the course of a single summer night, pop popcorn for her boys, watch a movie with them and then suddenly snap and turn into a knife-wielding nut?

A psychiatrist who interviewed Darlie for 14 hours after her arrest said that she was telling the truth about the attacks; that her loss of memory about certain details that night was the result of traumatic amnesia, which can occur after emotionally overwhelming events.

Vincent DiMaio, the chief medical examiner in San Antonio and the editor-in-chief of the prestigious *Journal of Forensic Medicine Pathology*, testified that Darlie's injuries were not at all consistent with the self-inflicted wounds he had seen in the past; he said that the cut across her throat, in particular, was hardly 'superficial', as the prosecutors alleged.

Mulder produced notes taken by the nurses at the hospital that said that Darlie was 'tearful', 'frightened', 'crying', 'visibly upset' and 'very emotional' on the night she was brought in.

However, countering this, one of the prosecution's expert witnesses aggressively promoted the theory that Darlie was guilty, and in the end the evidence, however circumstantial, was too much for the jurors – even if they could not figure out how the sock found its way into the alley.

During their deliberations, the jury watched the Silly String video a reported seven times.

Perhaps Mulder made a mistake in not introducing another videotape, secretly recorded by the police, that showed Darlie weeping over her sons' graves.

Perhaps the outcome would have been different had he found more expert witnesses to counter the prosecution's experts. But, even then, it's hard to see how a jury would have got over the finely honed image of Darlie as a mentally unbalanced, gum-chewing bleach blonde who seemed to be unmoved by, if not outright exhilarated over, the deaths of her children.

After the trial, it was proved that Darin Routier was looking for someone to burgle the house before the murders. 'Never,' Darin argued. But, according to an affidavit given by Darlie's stepfather, Bob Kee, Darin said in the spring of 1996 that he had a plan in which he and his family would be gone from the house and that a 'burglar', hired by him, would pull up with a U-Haul truck, remove household items and keep them hidden until the insurance company paid the claim. All that was needed, Darin said, was someone to do the job.

Initially, Darin poured scorn on the suggestion that he wanted someone to burgle his house to cash in on the insurance. But finally he had to admit that he had worked out another scam a couple of years before the murders in which he had had his car stolen so that he could collect the insurance money. Darin says that he did not arrange for his Jaguar to be stolen, but he admitted saying to the person who he believed eventually stole the car, 'It wouldn't bother me if it was gone.' Darin would not deny that the person who broke into his house and murdered his sons could have been someone who had heard him discuss his would-be insurance scam. But he said he had no idea who that person might be – and, if such a crime did happen, it was without his assistance.

'Why would I do that if I had my kids and my wife downstairs?' he said. 'That's the craziest story I have ever heard.'

When he was told that the complete truth might help get his wife a new trial, he insisted that he wanted to do what he could for Darlie. 'But I don't want to end up with some kind of bullshit charges brought against me either,' he volunteered. 'I don't want to help her at the expense of my life.'

But what if Darlie really did it and Darin was her accomplice in covering it up – a scenario that prosecutors say they have also considered?

What if Darin came downstairs, saw what his wife had done to the boys and then planted false clues to try to keep her from being arrested? Because he had no blood on him, he could have taken the sock down the alley without leaving a trail. He could have been the one who carefully cut Darlie's throat and inflicted her other wounds, after convincing her that the cops would be more likely to believe her story if she had also been stabbed.

Or maybe Darlie, who was in such a delicate emotional state only a month before, decided after one of her fights with Darin to murder the boys and then kill herself – only she couldn't quite bring herself to commit suicide.

What if Darin came downstairs, begged her to put the knife down and then planted false clues and staged a crime scene before having her call 911? Darin said all the speculation is outlandish, and that he still believes an unknown assailant came into his house. 'I love my wife and I loved my boys,' he has said. 'My God, I loved them. How did this ever happen?'

Proof of motive is not necessary in the proof of a crime, and the absence of any discoverable motive is of little consequence in deciding whether or not the prisoner committed the crime. Darlie Routier killed her children for whatever motive – murder for insurance was never one of them – and her guilt is overwhelming.

At the beginning, I asked the reader to stand back to look at a somewhat incomplete painting of homicide which had been designed to fool the eye. We then moved closer to examine how the exercise had been completed and learned much. Various areas of the canvas were missing or deliberately obscured by the perpetrator – all attempts to show us a picture that didn't really exist. A murderous *trompe l'oeil* indeed!

Yes, the couple had spats from time to time, but most couples have those and they make for healthy, open relationships. This couple were devoted to each other, despite the curtain-twitchers who claim otherwise. Of course, they might have discussed paying someone to rob their home for insurance purposes, but killing Darin, who was asleep close to Drake, for insurance reasons was the last thing on Darlie's mind.

The suicide note in Darlie's diary proves that she was falling apart at the seams a month before the murders. Her words are sad, and perhaps those of a sincere woman. But was this yet another warped way of getting attention, for she wrote the letter then telephoned her husband begging him to come home? When he did, she showed him the letter and he comforted her, giving her the reassurance she craved.

Darlie Routier was, and still is, a very materialistic woman with an underlying sense of low esteem. Her ego was fragile. To compensate for this, she indulged in expensive trinkets, clothes and other excesses, which others would describe as 'showy'. She dyed her hair to match the colour of her dog. She was an attention seeker who years beforehand had claimed she had been raped to gain the sympathy and attention of her peers. She had her breasts enlarged to a size that would outdo most raunchy centrefolds. All of this was a prop to support her own self-admitted inadequacies.

She knew there was no way out of the financial abyss into which they had plunged. They always say that a flame burns brightest before it goes out, and Darlie certainly burned bright, with high spirits, during the week before she killed her children. This was Darlie Routier to a T: showy on the outside, now a psychological wreck inside; a woman who needed sympathy and attention.

It was an inescapable fact that the Routiers were on the verge of bankruptcy. The IRS demanded hefty tax arrears. They owed their bank and credit card companies a small fortune. And the bank had refused them the lifeboat of a $5,000 loan. They would lose the house – all that they had worked so hard together for would soon be lost, probably for ever.

Darlie Routier once prided herself on her beautiful figure, but now she had put on weight she could not lose. She admitted to suffering from post-natal depression, her periods had stopped completely and, as every woman knows, the symptoms can become mentally debilitating. Society has witnessed time and again a parent killing their children in moments of deep despair.

Darin Routier is an extremely intelligent and mentally well-balanced man. His work in the electronic industry demands that he is methodical and thorough. Indeed, until he fell into financial difficulties, he was highly successful and motivated.

From their history together, we know that Darin was emotionally far better equipped to handle the family financial crisis than his materialistic and showy wife. Sadly, this case has the indelible stamp of 'familicide' writ large throughout.

Having filled in all of the missing pieces, I now suggest that Darlie Routier's mind had become a pressure-filling cylinder and the relief valve finally closed shut. In effect, her mind blew.

I do not believe that she had ever seriously considered suicide: she loved herself far too much to do that. The note and phone call to her husband were simply an attention-seeking exercise.

If there was a motive, as cold, dispassionate and brutal as this may seem, I believe that Darlie Routier killed her two sons and then mutilated herself to gain sympathy and attention as her materialistic world collapsed in ruins.

The murders were premeditated and the intruder scenario was hastily invented with little thought to careful planning, as has been proven. In all that followed the stabbings, we can picture a cold-blooded, calculating woman meticulously rearranging her home, taking care not to damage the items she held so dear to her heart: she could easily destroy her sons' lives, but not a spot of blood should contaminate the couch on which she slept or the flashy jewellery she wore.

Darlie Routier's latest hearing centred not on fingerprint evidence but on the thousands of errors made by the original trial stenographer. She and her internet supporters claimed that she could not receive a fair consideration of her appeal because the transcript was tainted. However, months of reconstructive work brought the transcript up to scratch, and on this basis the judge ruled against the appellant.

The rest is history, but the full picture certainly explains why the dog didn't bark in the night.

Inmate # 999220, Darlie Routier, is at Texas Department of Corrections, Mountain View Unit DR, 2305 Ransom Road, Gatesville, TX 76528, USA.

NANCY KISSEL: 'THE MILKSHAKE KILLER'

'A sham masquerading as the best marriage in the Universe.'

NANCY KISSEL IN AN EMAIL TO A FRIEND

'This case? It's better than a Hollywood movie.'

POLLY HUI, A REPORTER AT NANCY KISSEL'S TRIAL IN HONG KONG

Her husband's body was wrapped in plastic film and a sleeping bag and then rolled up in a carpet. Days later, Nancy Kissel hired four Chinese workmen to carry the bundle to a storeroom, coolly ignoring their complaints that it smelled like rotten fish.

According to their wealthy friends and work colleagues in the former British colony of Hong Kong, 41-year-old Nancy Kissel and her husband, Robert, 40, seemed to be the ideal couple.

They had three children: Elaine, June and son Reis. But the couple both had dark secrets: Robert scoured the internet in search of weird sex with gay men; Nancy had a younger lover and trawled the web for drugs with which to kill her husband.

New York-born Robert had been educated at the University of Rochester's College of Engineering and had an MBA degree from the Leonard N Stern School of Business at New York University. He worked as a Vice President of Research for Lazard Freres & Co from 1992 to 1997, before he and Nancy moved to Hong Kong in 1998 with the Goldman Sachs Group Inc, to head its distressed asset business in the wake of the Asian financial crisis. In 2000, he was hired out to Merrill Lynch's Global Principal Investment as managing director of the Asia-Pacific division.

Born in Minneapolis, Nancy Kissel attended the University of Minnesota. She married her husband in 1989. A small, petite woman with raven-black hair, and a prominent member of Hong Kong's Jewish community, she had owned her own photography business and carried out a string of volunteer activities, which included work for the Hong Kong International School – the $15,000-a-year school attended by two of the couple's three children.

The family lived in an expensive rented apartment within the Parkview complex, set into the lush green hills that overlook the harbour, and, according to Jane Clayton, Robert's sister, at the time of his murder Robert's estate was valued in the millions. The deceased held two life insurance policies in Hong Kong worth a total of US$1.75 million, as well as a personal insurance policy from the United States with a face value of about US$5 million. In 2003 the banker's annual income was US$175,000, not including the US$5.9 million he had amassed in bonuses in his three years with Merrill Lynch.

The principal beneficiary of Robert Kissel's will was his wife, Nancy. It stated that, if he died before his wife, his entire estate would go to her. If she died before him, the estate would be distributed as 20 per cent to his brother, 20 per cent to his sister, 20 per cent to his father-in-law, 20 per cent to his mother-in-law and 20 per cent among friends. There was a lot at stake.

In December 2002, Robert's sister Jane noticed that her sister-in-law had become distant during a skiing trip to Whistler, Canada. 'Nancy argued a lot with other people,' she said. 'I was very careful when I was with her.' Jane added, 'Nancy left the holiday without saying goodbye.'

For his part, Robert Kissel had recently returned from Bali, Indonesia, where he had undergone a back operation.

In January 2003, without Nancy's knowledge, the banker, suspecting that his wife was having an affair, installed E-blaster spy software on both her laptop and her home computer. The software tracked her emails and sent reports to a Hotmail account read by himself.

In March, Nancy Kissel and her children left Hong Kong to evade the SARS virus outbreak. Planning to stay away for several months, they moved to their holiday home in Stratton Mountain, Vermont, while Robert remained in Hong Kong long enough to continue his work, while at the same time monitoring his wife's emails. Then, in June, he hired the New York private investigation company Alpha Group to spy on his wife for 11 days and confirm her infidelity. This surveillance would cost Kissel US$25,000.

The investigation proved positive. PI Rocco Gatta confirmed

that Nancy Kissel was having a fling with a television repairman named Michael del Priore. Younger than Robert, Michael had a good physique and lived at a trailer park near the Kissels' Vermont home.

During two sessions of surveillance, Gatta noted that a blue van was parked discreetly near the Kissels' multi-million-dollar home. On each occasion, the vehicle would be parked either in a ditch or halfway up the long drive, out of sight of both the main road and the house. The driver of the van would take off in the middle of the night, without turning on the headlights until reaching the main road. The registration number of the van revealed the owner to be Michael del Priore, Nancy's lover.

Intercepted emails from the Romeo, which may be described as 'love letters', contained passages such as: 'I love it when you call my name, it makes me melt.' Other email exchanges between the lovers included small talk about their daily lives, food preferences and love talk in which they called each other 'Baby' and 'Honey'. In one email Nancy wrote, 'I think about you so much, Michael…' At one point Michael writes, 'I am going crazy… when customers ask me questions, I want to tell them, "Leave me alone, I am busy thinking about Nancy."'

After the all-clear for the SARS outbreak was given, Nancy returned to Hong Kong, but continued her relationship with Michael del Priore over the internet.

On 28 July 2003, Robert Kissel contacted Sharon Ser, a senior partner at attorneys Hampton, Winter and Glynn, to enquire about divorce proceedings and custody of his children. By late September, he had twice told Frank Shea, the owner of Alpha

Group Investigations, that he feared for his safety and suspected his wife of trying to poison him.

Robert discovered on 28 August that Nancy had indeed been searching the internet using keywords such as 'sleeping pills', 'overdose medication causing heart attack' and 'drug overdose'. He also told Shea that, when he returned home from work and had his usual glass of Scotch, he felt 'woozy and disorientated'. The investigator advised him to report to the police with blood and urine samples. Sadly, Robert did not heed the advice because he felt guilty for suspecting his wife.

This was a mistake that would cost him his life.

On 20 October, Fung Yuet-seung, an assistant in a clinic on Icehouse Street, gave Nancy Kissel a prescription for Stilnox, a short-term treatment for insomnia, and for the antidepressants Amitriptyline and Lorizan, all in tablet form.

Three days later, Nancy Kissel visited a doctor, who prescribed her ten tablets of Rohypnol, the so-called 'date rape' drug. That night she searched the internet for any contraindicative effects the drug might have.

Again, Robert spotted his wife's internet search and contacted Frank O'Shea, this time also confirming that Nancy had been using another mobile phone to communicate with her lover, and that he was again concerned about his safety.

Robert Kissel had told lawyer Roger Egerton that he had informed his wife about his suspicions that she was having an affair. Nancy seemed 'unfazed' when he showed her the telephone bills with the details of her television repairman lover in the US, and he explained to Egerton that he was going to discuss the divorce arrangements on the afternoon of 2 November.

But Robert was now doomed. It was the countdown for murder.

At Nancy Kissel's trial, the picture painted by the prosecution was one of ice-cold calculation on the defendant's part for the act of premeditated murder.

On Saturday, 1 November, Samantha Kriegel, an accomplished photographer and a member of the same United Jewish Congregation in Robinson Road as the Kissels, was asked to take some photos of the couple's children in the Parkview garden. 'At this time, everything seemed perfect,' said Kriegel, 'and the kids got on very well with me.'

The next day, Nancy Kissel went to the synagogue. Robert emailed his brother, Andrew, and one of his friends about his intention to divorce his wife.

Around 4pm – it may have been a little earlier but not much later – the Kissels' neighbour Andrew Tanzer and his daughter, Leah, called on them for the first time. Tanzer introduced Leah to Kissel's six-year-old daughter, June, suggesting that they get to know each other. The children wanted ice cream and took several containers from the freezer, but they decided to make sundaes instead, while Nancy prepared a milkshake.

All the children helped, with the girls in charge of peeling the bananas and the son breaking up the cookies. Since it was Halloween, they decided to add red and black food colouring to make a 'Halloweeny' milkshake. Robert came into the kitchen several times and rolled his eyes at the chaos that was going on.

Tanzer asked for a glass of water, but both he and Robert were offered the large pink milkshake, which Nancy said was 'a secret recipe'. The girls took the drinks to their respective fathers, who knocked them back in two gulps, and then Tanzer said his goodbyes and left with Leah. Tanzer would later describe the drink as 'a strange milkshake – fairly heavy, sweet, thickened...

with banana taste, crushed cookies, reddish, which I guess was from some strawberries or flavouring… I have never drunk something like this before.'

Later, Robert Kissel and his two-year-old son both drank the remainder of the milkshake from the blender, and at about 4.50 neighbour David Friedland spotted Robert playing with his son at the Parkview clubhouse. 'Bob was in a chair, with his feet up, on the phone,' said Friedland. The two men chatted for a moment, then the banker signalled 'OK' as a parting gesture.

Back at home afterwards, Robert was feeling woozy. He told his wife that he was going to divorce her, saying that it was a done deal and that he had been talking to the lawyers.

When Tanzer returned to his own flat, his wife, Kazuko Ouchi, noticed that he had a very red face and seemed overly sleepy. He seemed so ill she even considered calling for an ambulance. The strange symptoms 'continued well into the evening' and this worried her. Her husband had drifted in and out of consciousness. He talked incoherently and then turned into a 'temperamental baby' as he devoured three tubs of ice cream, then vomited over the furniture. When Tanzer awoke the next morning, he was 'confused about the events after he had drunk the milkshake'.

David Noh, a close friend and colleague of Robert Kissel, phoned Robert at 5pm that Sunday to remind him of a planned conference call later. Noh later claimed at Nancy Kissel's trial that during the conversation he thought Robert Kissel was 'vague, tired and sleepy. He started talking about export growth instead of real estate prices. It was bizarre. I found him strange. He was not responding to my questions. He sounded slow in his speech and very mellow.' But, Noh added, 'being good friends, I actually made fun of him'.

At 5.58pm, telephone records showed, the banker made one last call to his secretary, Moris Chan, about getting tickets for the Harbour Fest.

Seven-thirty came, and Robert Kissel missed his conference call. Shortly afterwards, he fell asleep. It was a sleep from which he would never wake, for Nancy Kissel crept into the master bedroom and bludgeoned her husband to death with a heavy double figurine.

She slept with his battered body that night and for two nights afterwards.

The following day, Nancy emailed a casual friend, Scott Ligerwood, a children's entertainer, whom she was meant to meet for coffee at the cafe at Repulse Bay, saying, 'My husband's not well, I need to take care of things. Sorry, I will be in touch soon.'

At 7am, Nancy Kissel told her maid Maximina Macaraeg, one of two Filipino sisters employed by the family, that her hand was bandaged because of an injury caused by the oven. She also told the maid not to clean the master bedroom for several days. Later that day, Kissel went on a shopping spree at the Tequila Kola furniture store. Wearing dark glasses and being extremely loud, she spent over HK$15,000 on carpets, bed covers, cushions and a chaise longue. The next day she would return and buy two carpets costing HK$27,120.

On 4 November, Nancy told a doctor that her husband had assaulted her two nights before. She showed Conchita Pee Macaraeg cuts and bruises, explaining that she had had a fight with her husband two days previously. Nancy then sent Maximina off to the Adventist Hospital to buy a Velcro belt, saying that her ribs hurt and that she had broken them after playing tennis at the Aberdeen Marina Club. When the maid returned, she was sent out again, this time to a hardware store in Stanley to purchase rope.

The following day, Kissel called the Parkview management office and spoke to the supervisor. She requested that four maintenance workers come to her apartment to help her haul a thick roll of carpet to a storage area. She paid them HK$500. When the maid noted that the roll seemed unusually bulky, Nancy said that it contained pillows and blankets. The workers said that it smelled like rotting fish.

On 6 November, Nancy Kissel and her father, Ira Keeshin, went to the police station to report that her husband had assaulted her on the night of 2 November after she refused a sexual demand from him. Barely hours after she had filed the claim, Robert's friend David Noh filed a missing-person report on the banker. At 10.50 that night, police investigators interviewed her at her apartment. Then they searched the storage area and found the body of Robert Kissel.

A subsequent search by CSI officers revealed four boxes containing bedding, tissues, pillows and clothing belonging to both Nancy and Robert Kissel – all of which were stained with blood. Forensic scientists later confirmed that the DNA of the blood matched that of Robert and that his wife's left thumbprint had been found on the duct tape used to seal the boxes. They found bloodstains and specks of brain tissue in the bedroom, and among the sealed boxes was a metal ornament comprising two figurines which had become detached from the metal base. Body tissue recovered from the ornament was confirmed as that of Robert Kissel. It had been used like a hammer.

The pathologist reported that there were severe lacerations to the right side of the head of the victim which resulted in 'massive spillage of brain substance'. Lab tests found in Kissel's stomach and liver five types of hypnotics and antidepressants that would have impaired consciousness during the attack.

Government toxicologist Dr Cheng Kok-choi said that never before had he encountered the combination of drugs found in the deceased's stomach: Flunitrazepam (Rohypnol), Lorazepam (Lorivan), Amitriptyline and salicylic acid, which he claimed could be a product of the chemical breakdown of aspirin. In the liver, Dr Cheng found Amitriptyline and Axotal – the second was not registered for use in Hong Kong and had been purchased by Robert Kissel in the US.

No sign of defensive injury was found on the body and a chemist found 'insignificantly low' amounts of alcohol.

Nancy Kissel was arrested at 2.41am on 7 November after having been taken to Ruttonjee Hospital for a check-up. The bespectacled woman was diagnosed as suffering from emotional distress and was trembling, crying and unable to speak. Doctors found abrasions on her lip, chest and knees. Her palms were red and there was bruising on her forearms and shoulders. Blood samples revealed she was suffering from muscle injuries resulting from vigorous exercise. However, the prosecution later argued that this was caused by the 'considerable effort in wrapping the body with the carpet and placing it into the rug'.

At Nancy Kissel's trial – of which Albert Wong, a newspaper reporter present in court, said, 'For us, this case is a throwback to the colonial era. It has all the ingredients our readers are interested in – money, murder, gwelos [Cantonese slang for white foreigners], lots and lots of money, and the internet' – it became apparent that her marriage was not a happy one. Nancy

Kissel accused her husband of being a heavy drinker, a cocaine user, tight with his money, a strict disciplinarian, a violent man who was into rough and crude sex. However, the couple's maids denied witnessing any brutality and confirmed that, far from being tight with his money, Robert Kissel was a 'thoughtful and loving father' and extremely generous.

It was obvious that Nancy Kissel was generous too. Favouring Conchita, she allowed her use of her ATM card with a $7,000 daily limit, took her on holidays and had given her a laptop computer, an Aberdeen Marina Club card and HK$30,000 to renovate her house in the Philippines. Maximina was not shown such trust or generosity, and did not accompany the family on holidays.

Denying the murder, Nancy claimed that her husband, fuelled on cocaine, had attacked her with a baseball bat because she refused him oral sex. She had picked up a heavy lead figurine to defend herself and had struck a glancing blow to Robert's head. The fight had continued until he collapsed on his bed and fell asleep. She said that she then left the apartment with her husband still alive.

A police surgeon saw that she had a swollen lip, bruises and swellings on her face, arms, legs and feet, with fractures in her lower right rib and left hand. The injuries, it was argued by the defence attorney and agreed with by prosecution witness Dr Li Wei-sum, were consistent with 'classic defensive injuries' inflicted when a person tries to fend off a blunt, hard instrument. When senior counsel asked, 'Someone can come off a rugby field or out of a boxing ring with damage to those muscles?' the doctor agreed.

The defence then produced Robert Kissel's wooden baseball

bat, suggesting that Nancy's injuries were consistent with her having fended off blows from this bat wielded by her husband. The bruises found on her body and dents in the metal base of the ornament, identified as the murder weapon, were inflicted by the baseball bat, claimed the defence. However, forensic testing proved that the bat and the ornament had never come into contact, but it seems certain that Robert Kissel used the bat to beat his wife before he fell unconscious.

When Dr Cheng was asked if his toxicology tests on the murdered man screened for cocaine, the doctor said that such tests would not have picked up evidence of cocaine, which, in any case, becomes immediately hydrolysed, or dissolved, in the stomach.

Pressing further, defence counsel Alexander King asked, 'Did you actually carry out a test to see if the hydrolysed products were present in the sample?'

'No,' Cheng replied, adding, 'There is no universal screening procedure that could detect everything under the sun.'

Nancy Kissel's computers soon came under scrutiny, and forensic science officer Cheung Chun-kit, from the Technology Crimes Bureau, examined them, recovering fragments of emails and website addresses from the accused's purple Sony Vaio laptop.

The scientist confirmed that, on 28 August, 2003, the words 'sleeping pills', 'overdose medication causing heart attack' and 'drug overdose' had been entered on the laptop, and that Nancy had spent several minutes browsing the addresses 'sleepingpills.net' and 'medhelp.org'. He also confirmed that the E-blaster spyware secretly installed on Nancy Kissel's laptop by her husband had forwarded the same search covertly to the deceased. Also recovered by Cheung Chun-kit were fragments of emails, one of which, sent to her lover, read, 'After having a private investigator firm follow me, are they going to be watching me forever? Hidden cameras, tapped phones. I recognize what the affair has done trust-wise.'

The court also learned that Nancy Kissel's laptop was used to browse Hong Kong Police Force's websites on missing and wanted persons some four days after her husband's death.

But, if Nancy was frequently using her machine, experts soon established that Robert Kissel was using his Dell desktop computer, and not just for work, for at the time when he was staying in Hong Kong, just days before a trip to Taiwan, it was used to search for websites relating to gay sex in Taiwan and other sexual services.

According to travel records, Nancy Kissel went to the United States in March 2003 to avoid the SARS outbreak in the territory. The travel records also confirmed that Robert Kissel stayed behind, but left for a three-day trip to Taiwan on Tuesday, 8 April.

Using a programme called Netanalyses, which is said to be employed by law-enforcement agencies in the USA and the UK, to open up Robert Kissel's computer files, it was shown that on 3 and 4 April he used the computer for about 90 minutes to search for gay porn sites, Taiwan female escort services and 'sex in HK'. Searches were also made for 'mpeg sex', 'hot male sex', 'Taiwan companions' and 'married and lonely in Hong Kong'. 'Twinks' and 'Actresses for Hire in Taiwan' were also among sites visited.

Jumping on this information, the defence team highlighted

the fact that 'sex in HK' produced six results. A search for 'sex in Taiwan' yielded 516,000 results.

Further probing of Mr Kissel's computer records revealed search engine entries such as 'anal', 'cocks', 'gay anal sex', 'bisexual' and 'male ass'. Some had been made over the three days before he flew out to Taiwan.

Defence counsel Alexander King also pointed out that Robert Kissel's computer had visited websites offering images of nude gay boys, black gay men, black males, 'ebony' men and free black gay porn.

Deleted files can be removed from a computer as unallocated clusters and can be converted back into web pages using Encase software, but Encase cannot determine from unallocated clusters the dates on which pages were viewed.

Still not satisfied, King rounded on the computer expert and, in a further effort to discredit the deceased, he said, 'We move to Europe now, and can you see a search for "Paris girls for Hire"?

'Yes,' Cheung said, and confirmed he could see searches were made for 'Paris and home masseuse', 'Massage in Paris France', 'Paris gay' and 'Paris gay massage'.

Indeed, Robert Kissel had been criss-crossing the planet: on 5 April 2003 he had conducted a search for female and bisexual escorts in Perth, Western Australia, and a photo gallery under the header 'male cock gay sex gay men'.

Clearly, Mr Kissel was a dark horse, most certainly into extreme sex as well as a user of both male and female prostitutes, and evidence of his continual visits to porn websites featuring anal sex was starting to suggest that Nancy Kissel's claim that her husband was sexually abusive towards her was correct.

But did Nancy's claim that her husband was also physically violent to her have any foundation in truth?

Extracted from Nancy's computer notebook was this email to her husband, dated Tuesday, 7 October 2003: 'You are still justifying your harsh action in the car with the kids by blaming it on me. You see Rob, at the end of the day it seems that I am the only one making the effort. I have shown you in many ways how I have been trying. But because of that fight and how uncontrollable you got in the car… How you are always telling me we won't fight in front of the kids… A fight and you give out an ultimatum… I still can't believe it… Is it how life is going to be? Who should be going to therapy? Whatever happens… to us? You never use those words any more ever.'

Slowly a picture began to emerge that the Kissels' marriage had not been a bed of roses for several years. Nevertheless, the couple had been by and large successful in keeping their domestic problems to themselves.

After giving birth to her eldest daughter in 1994, Nancy Kissel had to abandon her own career – she had been holding down three jobs at once to help support her husband – and her body weight increased to 150 pounds. At the time, Robert encouraged her to lose weight and found all sorts of strange techniques for this purpose. Nancy said that her breasts began to sag after giving birth, which made her husband dislike her. So their sex lives changed as Robert began to force her to do things that she would rather not do.

Nancy's character changed from buoyant to moderately depressive after the birth of her third child, Reis, in 1999.

It also emerged that there was some probability that Robert Kissel had been taking the sleeping drug Ambien for several months before his death. And the suggestion was made that he had been using cocaine for some time. He was certainly under massive stress, and new cocaine users often use the drug to help them work longer and harder, as well as to assist other activities in their lives.

There was also the question of how the same milkshake cocktail, served by Nancy to the two men, affected them so differently: Tanzer is a big man and was affected by the drink after just 15 minutes. Surely the drink would have had the same pharmacological effect on Robert Kissel? But it didn't. Kissel was still behaving quite normally an hour after ingestion, by which time his neighbour had passed out – all of which suggests that he had developed a higher resistance to many of the drugs forming the milkshake.

While the prosecution attempted to make light of the defence team's claim that Robert had been searching the web for porn and illicit gay sex, by countering that he had been merely searching for Barbie Dolls for his daughters, this cut no ice. His continuous searches for anal sex and male and female prostitutes clearly showed that his demands for rough, anal sex with his wife were rightly going unmet, so he would seek his pleasures elsewhere.

With her marriage falling apart, finding a new male companion that she could confide in outside the family circle provided mental relief for Nancy, and this considerate ear would soon become her lover. Robert soon grew suspicious and before long he found confirmation that his wife was having an affair. He decided to divorce her and demand custody of the three children.

Nancy Kissel now stood to lose everything.

At her trial, Nancy Kissel painted a black picture of her last few years with her husband. 'Our early married life in New York was exciting,' she said, 'but arguments were already developing because of Rob's use of cocaine. As a hard-working student, he relied on cocaine to get through the hours. He had a drug-dealing friend who would come round to the apartment and money would exchange across the table.'

But the new job, in Hong Kong, illustrated the cumulative nightmare of stress, alcohol and cocaine – the last of which Robert Kissel allegedly relied on to stay awake as he worked both the US and Hong Kong stock markets. 'It's literally 24 hours of having to be awake,' said Nancy. 'On the flight to Hong Kong from New York, he passed out for 15, 20 minutes, probably from drugs, alcohol, altitude and jet-lag. After that incident, instead of shying away from the stress, he thrived on it. It's what made him tick – the power of it all, succeeding. Everything was based around money.'

Nancy testified that things really changed after she gave birth to their youngest child, Reis. She claimed that Robert had developed a routine of 'going home, drinking and sex'.

She claimed that the first time he hit her was when he realised that the expected birth of Reis would overlap with an important business trip to Korea. He told her to try to induce labour and was angry when she didn't listen to him. 'The first time he punched at me, he hit the wall because I dodged. When it happened again for the same argument the following week, he hit me on the face,' she said.

Nancy Kissel said that the first punch was so hard it broke through the surface of the wall. She knew he had broken his hand because the next day he came home with a plaster on his hand.

This much was confirmed by Dr Daniel Wu of Adventist Hospital, who told the court that he had treated the deceased's 'boxer's fracture' on his right little finger around August 1999.

After Reis was born, Nancy testified, her husband became more forceful with her during sex. 'It was predominantly oral sex for him and anal sex,' she said. 'He would be sitting on the end of the bed watching TV whenever he was at home at night. He would not let me walk past him to my side of the bed. He would start those games... having me between his legs, toying with me. He would say those things to me that he could do anything he wanted. He was just so angry... It was like I wasn't even there... he never had a look at my face.'

'Were you agreeable to that?' asked Alexander King.

'No,' Kissel replied. 'I often had bruises and bleeding from the anal sex forced upon me.'

She also told of two occasions when her ribs were fractured after Robert tried to twist and flip her over on the bed for anal sex. When it happened the first time, in 2001, she sought treatment at Adventist Hospital and was given a Velcro brace to wear around her stomach. 'A couple of weeks later, he ripped the brace off and I ended up getting into hospital again,' she said.

When asked about the family's finances, Nancy told the court that when they first arrived in Hong Kong her husband didn't care about her finances. But from 2002 he began to control her expenses, reducing the number of her credit cards from four to two. If she needed cash, she had to show the shopping list to him for approval. The defence pointed out, when Robert Kissel worked at Merrill Lynch between 2000 and 2003, his bonuses amounted to three million dollars.

It was inevitable that Nancy's relationship with Michael del

Priore would be brought up at her trial. In 2000, he had wired the family's home in Vermont for security and entertainment, but it was not until 2003, when she stayed longer in Vermont with her children, that she really came to know him.

She had regarded Michael, and the family's Vermont home, as a type of temporary shelter. She agreed that she had written in her diary that Michael offered her unconditional love, but she had added that her real world was the home she had built with her husband in Hong Kong.

In mid-June, Nancy and Michael spoke about tattoos, something she always wanted, but her husband thought 'corporate bankers' wives' should not have them. Del Priore took her to a tattoo parlour, then after dinner she opened up to him about the stress of trying to lead a perfect life as a banker's wife.

'[Michael] was very open and honest to me about his childhood,' she said. 'His mother was abused by his father and that he had alcoholics in the family. He noticed that this summer I looked like "shit", compared with the previous year, and had the same look as his mother did, which concerned him.'

'I broke down and cried,' she said. 'It was the first time anybody ever stepped forward and confronted me on an issue that scares a lot of people. People look at you and see change, and they don't really want to know.'

Nancy testified that she had felt she could finally confide in someone about the 'little expatriate world', where people are 'more interested in what you're wearing and how big your diamond ring is and your car'. By contrast, with Michael there were 'no questions, no "do this, do that". It was just basically letting me talk.' The relationship continued mostly through phone calls and emails, and involved three sexual encounters.

During a skiing holiday in Whistler in 2002, Nancy told the court that her husband was 'embarrassed' that she could not ski, despite the fact that she thought looking after their sick two-year-old son Reis was more important.

On Christmas Eve, he thought she was fussing over the Christmas tree for too long. 'He grabbed me from downstairs and pulled me upstairs, because he wanted what he wanted. And I let him. And then I went back downstairs and finished with the presents,' she said, 'which angered him more because he had told me not to. Then he slammed me against the wall.'

When asked about her internet searches for sleeping pills and information on medication causing heart attack, Nancy broke into tears, explaining that she had attempted to kill herself one night when the maid had left and the children were asleep. 'I sat in the car in the garage and turned the engine on. I cried a lot. Maybe I got scared of leaving my children, so I turned the engine off and went back into the house.'

She told the jury she searched the internet for information on 'sleeping pills', 'medication causing heart attack' and 'drug overdose' in August 2003 because she was again contemplating suicide.

One of the triggers for this, during a trip to New York they made that month, was that her husband had forbidden her to pick up their eldest daughter, Elaine, from a camp in Maine. She had been ordered to return to Hong Kong, while Robert and his father, William, would pick Elaine up.

'I thought if I am going to do something like this, taking pills, I wouldn't want my children to be affected – going through the knowledge of their mother committing suicide.'

Asked if she had at any time spiked her husband's whisky,

Nancy readily agreed that she had. She told the court that her husband was using cocaine, painkillers and whisky – this much was confirmed – and she said that she was worried when she realised that his violence had spilled over to hurt the children. He once got angry with Elaine for not eating vegetables in Vermont. 'He printed photographs of malnourished people – which she hated – grabbed her, kept shaking her and jumped on her. She said, "Daddy, you are hurting me," but he just kept shaking her.'

So Nancy put sleeping pills in Robert's bottle of whisky in an attempt to calm him down, 'but it had little effect on him'.

By now, it appeared that Robert was controlling every different aspect of Nancy's life. He told her to stop phoning her father in America, which she did every day, and to stop doing volunteer work for their daughters' school. And he was furious when he discovered she had returned from Vermont with a tattoo on her shoulder, reminding her that she was a banker's wife.

On Wednesday, 3 August 2005 in court, Nancy Kissel was asked to detail the events leading up to the death of her husband. Dressed completely in black and trembling uncontrollably, she said that she was caught completely by surprise when Robert told her he was divorcing her. 'He said I've filed for divorce and I'm taking the kids. He said it's a done deal and he'd talked to lawyers. He said I was in no condition to look after the kids and that I was sick.' She said that he later hit her when she started questioning him. He then dragged her into the bedroom and forcibly sodomised her.

'He grabbed my ankles and pulled me and wouldn't let go... He said I'm not finished with you yet,' she testified, her voice shaking and barely audible. 'He kicked me in the stomach and he wouldn't stop… I was on the floor and I reached for the statue and swung it back at him. I felt I hit something and he let go… I saw his head was bleeding … and he said, "I'm going to kill you."'

She said he then hit her repeatedly with a baseball bat as she swung at him with the metal ornament. As for what happened afterwards, Nancy told the court she had no recollection. The autopsy found that Robert Kissel had sustained five fatal blows on the side of his head, but his wife had no recollection of hitting him five times.

Nancy Kissel was found guilty of murder and sentenced to life imprisonment.

The drugs found in the stomach of the decomposing body of Robert Kissel were prescribed for Nancy, who was struggling to sleep for fear of his violent sexual whims.

At the end of August 2003, Nancy had gone to see Dr Fung, a psychiatrist, because she was physically and mentally exhausted owing to the 'inconsistency of not knowing' when the sexual abuse would occur and having an 'on-guard feeling all the time'. She was prescribed Stilnox, Amitriptyline and Lorivan – three of the sedatives later found in her husband's body.

It is obvious, when one considers the timing of her internet searches for sleeping pills and medication that could cause heart attacks, that Nancy Kissel was looking for a means to commit suicide. As for the Rohypnol? On the morning of 23 October 2003, she had been prescribed this expensive drug by Dr Annabel Dytham. Not knowing what the drug was, she had searched the internet that evening for details.

'I just wanted to talk to her [Dytham] as a woman,' she said. She explained everything about her husband – the physical and sexual abuse; that her life was 'pretty miserable'.

The doctor wrote in her notes: 'Alleged assault.'

In her efforts to bring peace to the family home, Nancy attended marriage-counselling sessions, after which her husband accused her of wasting time and money by 'not listening', and then violently sodomised her to encourage her to 'show more respect'. He told her how much the sessions were costing and asked what she was contributing to the marriage, before sexually assaulting her again.

During the second counselling session she told him that she was going to divorce him. The banker stormed out and returned home at 2am the next morning, drunk and angry. Bursting into the bedroom, Nancy says, he started yelling at her, 'Who do you think you are, asking for a divorce like that? You'll never divorce me. If anyone's doing the divorcing around here, it'll be me.'

Nancy Kissel emphatically denies making the milkshake with a cocktail of sleeping pills, and still maintains that she hasn't a clue how the drugs came to be in the drink. She supports this contention by saying, 'I love my kids, I would never harm my kids, or anyone else's kids. I would never make a drink like that to hurt them.'

At face value, this seems a good argument. However, the children made up large enough measures to make sundaes for themselves and milkshakes for their fathers, and it was just the milkshakes that Nancy drugged.

There can be no doubt that, after Robert told his wife he was divorcing her and was taking custody of the children, the Kissels had a furious row that evening. I believe that Robert, now realising that he had been drugged, and in some fear, struck out at his wife with the baseball bat, striking her several times before collapsing on his bed.

Nancy Kissel, by now at the end of her tether, waited until he was completely unconscious, then took up the ornament and hit him over the head five times.

SUSAN GRAY AND 'THE FEATHERMAN'

'I had never had a climax in my life until I met "The Featherman" on the internet. We met, he raped me and returned to almost kill me.'

SUSAN GRAY, TO THE AUTHORS

As most people will agree, the feeling of emptiness when one has been rejected by a loved one may be misinterpreted as a need to go shopping, or as a need to eat. The need for companionship and love and the sense of loss that is now associated with this need may be too painful to scrutinise consciously. The person engages in unrelated behaviour that results in a temporary reduction of the feelings associated with loneliness and tends to bring pleasure. Feeling good about one thing masks the pain being felt elsewhere.

We will soon learn a lot about Susan Gray (not her real name) and how, spurned by three husbands, she found herself in an internet chatroom unknowingly talking to a sexual predator. We will learn even more about the man himself – and it is a story that provides a salutary lesson to women looking for relationships in the chatrooms of the world.

Susan Gray, and at least two other British women, fell for a smooth-talking American on the internet. During a five-week visit he raped all of them – there were probably others too – and Susan almost lost her life. Later in this book we encounter two men, a London doctor and a US mechanic, who did.

Susan was born 47 years ago in Maidstone, Kent. Today a tall, natural blonde with blue eyes, she could readily be described as 'classy' and 'hot stuff', and the combination of her slim figure with sexy clothes, short skirts and high-heeled black boots has always drawn admiring glances from men and women alike.

Intelligent, house-proud and generous to a fault, Susan has a teenage son, although, sadly, by the age of 40 she had three failed marriages behind her.

'I guess I was a bit possessive,' she explained. 'Maybe I was insecure knowing that my husbands and other lovers knew that I was not getting sexual satisfaction from the relationships. I don't understand it at all, but I admit I was a bit of a control freak and very jealous.' She added, 'Yes, I have always been generous to my men. Perhaps I was trying to buy their love. I seem to have attracted the wrong men.'

Susan was always on the move – and she still is. Unable to put down roots as each relationship fell apart, she would diligently pack all of her possessions into cardboard boxes and find somewhere else to live. Gradually, almost step by step, she gravitated to Fareham in Hampshire, where she shared rooms with two other girls above a cafe in West Street.

Within 18 months, Susan moved again, then again, and then, in 2001, she rented a two-bedroomed cottage in Emsworth, in the same county. The former coach house with its ivy-covered wall-enclosed garden, she decorated tastefully. Now unattached, she started working as a sales and promotion agent for a national company. With her winning ways, she was soon easily earning £900 a week with commission.

Susan prided herself on her cooking and loved entertaining so before long she had splashed out £1,000 on a dinner service and new cutlery. She discarded her old wine glasses and bought new ones. A new dining table and chairs followed, then she treated herself to a new wardrobe.

Now settled in, she took stock of her life. The cottage was cute, with a cosy lounge, a proper fire, a dining room where Susan had her computer workstation and a kitchen looking on to the garden. A narrow staircase with a low beam – 'one has to mind your head,' she said when we visited her – led to the two bedrooms. The only inconvenience was the location of the shower room and toilet, which was reached via the kitchen – a small price to pay for such an idyllic home.

Susan's daily routine was simple. She would work five days a week, occasionally on a Saturday, then shop for dinner, after which she would stroll down to the seafront and take in the air. On Sundays she made a point of feeding the swans on the nearby millpond, then driving over to see her mother for lunch.

In June 2001, a girlfriend, Carol, called on Susan, bringing a few bottles of wine. After dinner, she introduced her host to the website of Absolute Agency. Carol was a regular visitor to the site's chatroom and she told Susan that perhaps they could have 'a little fun'.

Although she had a high-speed internet connection, Susan had never visited a site like this before and indeed said, 'It would have been the last thing on my mind at the time because I believed that people who use chatrooms have no real lives.'

Within the hour and after much more wine, Susan was persuaded to log on to the site. Egged on by her friend, who seemed to know a few of the people who used it, she submitted a profile and photograph. Membership was free for women – for obvious reasons – and she became hooked. Susan chose the name 'Susie Q' and selected a female avatar with blonde hair.

'I remember that night very clearly,' Susan says. 'All of those people chatting away with each other. But from the moment I logged on the men spotted a new face and I had a swarm of them asking me questions. They were like bees around a honey pot and it clearly upset a number of the other girls who were online.'

The one male icon and name that attracted Susan above the others was an American called 'The Featherman'. 'He was very funny, sort of cute and sexy,' she remembers. 'The other females liked him a lot, and he teased them along with a few of his male pals in there. His name conjured up the image of a "cheeky little duck". He was always saying that ducks like water and bubbles, and would anyone like to join him in the bath? It was kind of cute… I expect this sounds crazy. Anyone reading this will say I am mad.'

Carol explained that this guy was very popular. He was a regular and a fully paid-up member – meaning in chatroom parlance that he had 'cyber cred'. Most of the other males could chat for only 15 minutes because they had not paid to join up.

'This means "The Featherman" is a serious player,' Carol explained. 'Full members are the elite. You get to know the serious guys and they kinda stick together like a club.'

'The Featherman' was intelligent and his chat was not overtly sexual. His humour was dry and all of this, combined with his cheeky little duck image, attracted Susan to him.

Over the coming days, she spent ever-longer periods in the chatroom, and she admits that she started to rush home early from work and immediately logged on to the site to see if 'The Featherman' was there.

'I would feel a pang of disappointment if he was not around,' she said. 'I would ask the other members if he had been in earlier, or if anyone knew when he would be back. When he did turn up, I competed for his attentions. Looking back now I realise that I was becoming hooked on this chatroom and, this may sound stupid, but I was falling in love.'

Then she made a very interesting comment: 'When a woman has been rejected so many times, you start thinking too much about yourself and where you are going wrong. My ego was at an all-time low. "The Featherman" cheered me up and I felt somehow wanted again.'

The man then emailed his photograph to Susan, and she returned a number of pictures of herself. They also exchanged phone numbers. He was a little shorter than her five feet nine inches, thinning on top and he had a cheeky smile. Now using his real name, Bill, he informed her that he was single and had never been married. He was a pipeline consultant who travelled the world. All of this was true. He could be away from the USA for months, he told her, while at other times he worked from an office at his home in Augusta, Georgia. Photos of his house with its manicured lawns, and of a smart white car, showed that he was a neat and tidy man – an ideal catch for any woman.

'Because of the time difference between our two countries, Bill usually logged on around 10.30pm our time,' Susan said over dinner. 'I could understand that basically he was very much a man's man, well travelled and a guy who kept himself to himself. He wasn't flashy, or anything like that. This is why he appealed to me. We were very much like-minded, I think.'

She could never have guessed that her 'ideal catch' was at the same time using other chatrooms to stalk and groom several other women from the UK.

Knowing that Susan seriously fancied him, in the chatroom Bill offered just her a Mars Bar. 'You can play with this however you want,' he suggested. This offer drew some lewd comments from the other 'chatterers' who were vying for his attention.

'It was so sweet of him,' Susan recalled. 'A Mars Bar may sound pathetic, but it was a nice thought… a sexy one at that.

'After that, we often went into the Private Lounge area of the site, where we could chat discreetly. Often it got pretty sexual, and when we returned to the common area people would demand to know where we had been. Several of the other girls would get very bitchy.'

Susan then told us about some of the other 'chatterers'. 'There was a guy from Washington called "InsultBot". His avatar was an aggressive face with a biker's cap. It fitted with his rude and blunt attitude … he seemed always spoiling for a fight. "Wicked Maiden" was a female American cop from New York. She was heavily into Bill, and chains and whips. There were dozens of them from all over the world. Homosexuals, bisexuals and lesbians. Some were decent, most were lonely people, others were just filthy perverts.'

Bill and Susan had known each other for about three months. They regularly wrote each other long emails and when he asked her to buy a webcam she did.

'By then, Bill had become a major part of my life. I felt good because he spent most of his chatting time with me,' she recalled. 'I got very jealous when he teased the other girls, or talked to them. I wanted him all to myself. So, when he asked me to get a camera and microphone, I readily agreed.'

From then on the cyber couple talked about their aspirations for the future. She used the webcam to show him her dining room and he did likewise, showing her his office. Then they started to engage in cyber sex. Bill would tell Susan what he wanted her to wear, and during the sessions she would use a Mars Bar to satisfy herself while he masturbated.

During the fourth session she climaxed for the first time in her life.

'You know this is all very silly,' she said, clearly embarrassed. 'Strangely enough, I was not at all shy with him. He told me that he hadn't had a girlfriend for years and I wanted to please him as much as possible… The climax? It was fantastic!

From there, things got hotter between them.

'He would hint at a subject, just to see what my reaction would be. It was like he was fishing,' Susan explained. 'For instance, he would talk about mirrors, or ask what my thoughts were on blue movies. He asked if I had ever watched them, and I said, "Yes!" Sexy mags? All that stuff. When we were hot enough we would do cyber sex, then wash and return to chat about a future – maybe together.'

Looking back on this now, Susan agrees that she was being groomed. 'It was so subtle. So clever. He pretended to tease me, or ask my opinion about sexual issues. I enjoyed it because he knew when not to mention sex and, when he did, his timing was perfect.'

In early September, Bill told Susan that his business required that he visit Wales for a few weeks. From there he said he would travel on to the Middle East, but this second claim turned out to be a lie. She suggested that he might like to visit her in Emsworth and stay over. 'The Featherman' accepted the offer immediately and a date was set. He would arrive five days earlier than planned to spend time with her. She would drive to Heathrow Airport to collect him in her car.

On Thursday, 27 September, Bill Chandler (name changed for legal reasons) arrived in the UK. Wishing to make a good impression, Susan met him wearing an expensive, revealing leather top which accentuated her full breasts, a short leather skirt and a pair of knee-length black boots which she had recently bought in Milan while on a free trip she had won as top salesperson for her sales region. With her long, natural golden hair, she must have been a knockout and undoubtedly would have taken the man's breath away.

'I have never felt so nervous in my life,' she says. 'The plane was a bit late, too. But when he walked through arrivals he looked at me, blew me a kiss and within moments he hugged me tight and kissed my cheek.'

When they arrived at her cottage after a two-hour drive, she freely admits, 'We were as hot as hell. He was the perfect gentleman and we exchanged gifts and opened a bottle of Champagne as soon as we got in the door.'

She had bought him two bath towels that had little ducks on the corner. She even got him a toothbrush and emptied one of her drawers for his clothes.

Within the hour they were in bed. Susan had complied with one of her cyber lover's fantasies and had had large mirrors attached to the wall at the head, to the foot of the bed and to the ceiling.

'I lit candles by the bed… wrote "I Love You" in lipstick on the mirrors, and left a little paper trail into my spare room – squares of paper with arrows – to a place where I had hidden an expensive watch which I bought him in Italy… I even set the time for Georgia…'

At this point as we talked, Susan became visibly upset. She was clearly a warm-hearted woman who was thinking back to what might have been.

For 20 minutes we left her to clear away the plates, allowing her time to compose herself. She lit the fire and after a while she apologised, then carried on.

'All those months of wanting him. His accent was fantastic. He just drove me crazy in bed for hours. He was insatiable. It was all so romantic. Crazy, stupid, but so romantic.'

The day after he arrived they went sightseeing. Susan took him to 'real English pubs for real English beer'. They went to Portsmouth, took long drives into the country, visited Arundel Castle, did the movies and dined out. 'We went Dutch at my insistence,' she says, 'although he wanted to pay for everything.'

Clearly, Susan was in love. 'He loved my little cottage. He loved the swans and I took photos of him with them so he could show his friends back home. He died for the English food… got friendly with people in a local pub. He fitted in straight away. I just felt so good with him. Oh, shit. Oh, *fucking shit!*'

On their fifth and last night in bed, Susan agreed to his suggestion that he tie her up for sex and take a few sexy photographs. 'I trusted him completely,' she says. 'He was adventurous, strong, quite dominant, but I felt safe with him. I wanted him to leave with the need to come back. I wanted to please him; after all it is not often that a busy professional man travels halfway around the world to spend time with a woman he has only met in cyberspace… least of all me. I was flattered… You know, I had his home address, his email address, his phone numbers… He even asked me if I would consider moving to the USA, or said that he could easily get a job with his company here.'

Bill tied Susan's wrists together and lashed them over her head to the top of the bed. He then pulled up her black leather skirt, spreadeagled her legs and secured her ankles.

The authors feel that it would be gratuitous to detail what took place other than to report that Bill then attacked her, and what followed was a rape of terrifying proportions. Susan says she was helpless under this onslaught from the powerful man. She felt a hand gripping at her throat, tighter and tighter. Her gasp for air was cut off.

'You frustrated bitch,' he snarled. 'You want to be fucked like a whore and used like a fucking whore?'

Her fingers scrabbled to release his grip. Her eyes started to bulge, and then he slapped her hard across the face, chipping a front tooth.

Bill Chandler subjected Susan to a three-hour ordeal. Then he suddenly stopped and apologised. He untied her restraints and led her in a state of emotional and physical collapse downstairs to the shower, where he washed her and dressed her cuts.

An hour later, 'The Featherman' ordered a taxi to take him to London. As he walked out of the door, he said, 'If you call the police, I shall show them evidence of the whore you truly are. I have all your emails and photographs. Just say nothing and be pleased, 'cos I may come back again.'

Two weeks later the rapist phoned Susan from Cardiff. 'He was very, very apologetic,' she said during our interview. 'He told me that he had never done anything like this before… that my body and clothes brought out the Devil in him… that he loved me desperately and then, with a cheeky laugh, he asked if I could scrub his back again.'

Bill sent her 20 red roses via Interflora, and Susan explained that during the several phone calls that followed she forgave him. He said that he was so ashamed of himself he had cancelled his trip to the Middle East and wanted to see her again for just one night to patch things up.

She agreed.

'You will think that I was mad,' she said. 'I *was* mad. But when you have a guy who appears to be crying down the phone, begging forgiveness… Um… the flowers with a little card… Then when he laughs and says something like, "Hey! You shouldn't have been so sexy, babe," it throws you.'

It was then that good luck – if it could be called good luck – intervened. The following evening, expecting Bill to turn up around 7pm the next day, Susan checked her emails and logged on to the Absolute Agency site intending to say 'Hi!' to everyone and leave. Almost immediately, she saw 'The Featherman'. He was talking to another woman who she knew came from Poole in Dorset.

'I was shocked,' she said. 'Then they both went off the screen for the night. I tried to phone Bill, but he would not answer my calls or SMSs. I was numb.'

Then anger, mixed up with a kind of jealousy, kicked in. She sent Bill a message telling him that all deals were off and that she was going away for a few days. She didn't want to see him again.

During a sleepless night, Susan had a premonition that 'The Featherman' would turn up anyway, so she arranged to visit her mother and return home about midnight. She reasoned that, if he did turn up, as previously agreed, and found she was out, he would go on his way.

She was wrong.

Bill Chandler had indeed arrived at the cottage around 7pm and, so confident was he that Susan would be there, he sent the taxi driver off before he had even opened the garden gate.

'I will never forget what happened that night for the rest of my life,' said Susan. 'I got home about 11.30. It was pouring with rain and the place was in darkness. I walked through the garden and let myself in. I went to the kitchen to get a drink and when I looked out of the window I saw a man sitting on the seat under my apple tree. He just sat there and said nothing. I must have passed within feet of him and never saw a thing.'

Susan says she was very scared, and pretended she hadn't seen him. Shaking with fear, she went to go to bed and then he tapped on the front door – the only door to the cottage. She ignored him. Then he called out to her several times, softly at first, then the taps became knocks and his voice grew louder.

Then he kicked the door.

'Will you open this fuckin' door, please? Just to *fuckin' talk*.'

Although by now terrified, Susan plucked up the courage to tell him to go away.

'He started hammering on the door with his fists,' she said. 'He kicked and kicked the door until I thought he would smash it down. Then I called 999 and asked for the police to come quickly as I had an intruder on the premises.'

Alone, in a cottage at night! No one knows what one would do under such frightening circumstances, so one cannot blame Susan for the actions that followed. She says that, safe in the knowledge that the police were on their way, and concerned about more damage being done to the door of the rented cottage, she called out to him to stop. Leaving the phone off the hook so that the operator could hear what was going on, she released the lock to reason with Bill. She was greeted with a punch to her face that sent her reeling backwards across her front room. She fell, hitting her head on a coal scuttle.

Susan screamed and screamed.

'Within seconds he was in,' she said. 'Trying to grab my throat and hitting me. I told him the police were coming. He kicked me several times. He spat at me. His language was evil. Then he walked off.'

Emsworth is a small, conservative place where crime is rare. For this reason, emergencies in and around the village are attended by police based some 20 miles away, in either Chichester or Cosham, a northern suburb of Portsmouth. Unless a traffic policeman is patrolling the vicinity, response times can be up to ten long minutes.

In this case, the switchboard operator was dealing with a situation that could turn into a murder. Officers were galvanised into action and two police vehicles arrived within four minutes of Susan's call. No fewer than six other units sped into the village. However, because the cottage adjoined other dwellings and stood within a fully enclosed walled garden it could only be accessed by a gate at the end of a little-used alleyway. It would take anxious officers another three vital minutes to gain entry.

Susan was bleeding. She was hysterical and a female police officer spent an hour trying to settle her down. An ambulance was called, but her injuries were not severe and the medics treated her on the spot.

Meanwhile, Emsworth was swarming with police, and with only two main roads out of the community it was not long before Chandler was spotted. He was arrested at 1.35am trying to thumb a lift. He spent the night at Cosham Police Station while a statement was taken from Susan Gray.

'I thought about it all that night,' she said. 'I knew that he would say that I had encouraged him and that he had photographs and emails recording our dates and chats on the internet. Our sex, the mirrors. It would all come out in court and be in the papers, so I did not press charges.'

Bill Chandler was released from police custody without charges being pressed. Subsequently, it was reported that he had attacked and raped a 26-year-old woman in Wales. Later, Susan said that he had raped an 18-year-old clerical worker from Poole.

We don't know the name of Miss 'A' from Cardiff. South Wales Police did receive a complaint from a teenager who was admitted to hospital after being raped and beaten by an American man answering Bill Chandler's description. However, the young woman also refused to press charges, and as far as the police were concerned there was nothing more they could do.

Accompanied by Susan Gray, Christopher Berry-Dee met Miss 'B' from Poole. The two women had much in common, including the fact that neither had known that Chandler was stalking the other. At the time, Miss 'B' worked for a large insurance company in the town and lived with her parents.

'Yes! I met him [Chandler] in AA. Yes! He was much older than me. Yes! He raped me in my car. Me and Susan have talked about him often. He pulled the same dirty stunt on me... There is not much more I want to say because my parents had warned me many times about meeting someone just a bit younger than my dad.'

Asked how this sickening experience had affected her life, she said, 'What do you think? I have a steady boyfriend now... he doesn't know anything. I still shake when I switch on my computer because I know Chandler is there somewhere. I would never do chat again. It is like he would be there watching me. Twisted bastard!'

Robert Jensen, Associate Professor of Journalism at the University of Texas at Austin, writes: 'We live in a culture in which rape and battery continue at epidemic levels. And in this culture, men are masturbating to orgasm in front of television and computer screens that present them sex with increasing levels of callousness and cruelty toward women. No matter how hard it may be to face the reality of a rape culture, at least the culture still brands rape as a crime. Pornography, however, is not only widely accepted but sold to us as liberation. We know relatively much about how violent pornography influences ordinary adult men. There are negative influences on men's attitudes towards woman. After reception of violent pornography men become more positive to rape and evaluate women more callously. All too often, rape leads to murder.'

West Sussex Police, like their colleagues in South Wales, say,

'We treat all complaints of this nature very seriously. Unfortunately, if the victim feels unable to make a formal statement there is little we can do.'

The FBI are a little more encouraging. 'We do know Mr Chandler. He has a minor criminal record in the US. If the British Police have evidence that this man has committed serious sexual offences, we would be grateful for this information, and he could be extradited to stand trial in the UK.'

The FBI also say, 'Many sexual predators stalk their victims over a period of time. They do it in the real world and now they use the internet. They often gain more sexual satisfaction from the stalking phase than actually committing the offence. To them stalking is control. It gives these people a feeling of power. We are unable to comment on the allegations made against Mr Chandler… it seems that the three English women you mention are the victims of a very sick serial rapist. This man will continue to rape until he is arrested and charged. Failing that, undoubtedly he will commit murder, if he hasn't already done so.'

Susan Gray believes that Chandler might have killed her. She no longer dates anyone, but she visits Miss 'B' frequently. And Susan has seen 'The Featherman' on the internet since her ordeal.

'I know his line of chat,' she confirmed. 'He still uses the AA site but under a different name. I have tried to warn the girls but they don't believe me. They think I am a jealous crank. One guy said, "Prove it, you sad bitch." Several women, whom I knew from before, told me that I was a liar. I even emailed one of them a photo of me and Bill together. She replied, "He can fuck me any time," so I don't bother any more.'

The authors asked Susan if she had any advice for women using chatrooms and the internet to find sex or love.

Her reply was diplomatic. 'I would say be very careful. I suppose there are a lot of happy couples out there where things have worked out OK. But this experience has wrecked my life.'

Susan Gray has since moved from Hampshire.

The Ukraine-based Absolute Agency now monitor their chatroom. Although they can ban visitors who frequently use expletives, they admit that there is *nothing* they can do to stop scammers or prevent the likes of Bill Chandler from looking for prey. In a statement to the authors, they confirm, 'We now have a system which is called IGNORE. People can make someone invisible if they want. If we receive many complaints we terminate full membership and there is no refund. We even will ban the same person if he rejoins because we keep email addresses on file. We are not in the business of mind reading. We are in business for bringing people together and money.'

Indeed they are!

Eighty per cent of Ukrainians cannot afford bread every day. Fifteen per cent of the population are considered 'upper-class', meaning they earn as much as $30,000 a year. The remainder are mega-rich, and we invite you to consider the sums below.

Absolute Agency is the largest online dating/marriage business in the world. It is a major operation, with another office in Lithuania, and publishes at least 52,000 female profiles and 32,000 male profiles at any one time, with thousands of new profiles added each month. It has a chatroom and video streaming linked to hardcore pornography and prostitution. Absolute Agency has links with thousands of other sites that spread around the globe and the income derived from its business places it at the top of the business league in Ukraine – and one nameless man owns it all.

While it would be fair to say that the majority of their profiles are genuine, countless thousands are not, for lurking among their members are mafia scammers, countless seriously deranged people and sexual deviants, including paedophiles, serial rapists and stone-cold killers. Log on and, if you are a woman, soon they could be stalking you.

Absolute Agency can buy whatever and whomever they want. I was cordially invited to visit their offices but I respectfully declined, hopefully remaining on cordial terms.

DR ROBERT JOHNSON: MISSING, PRESUMED DEAD!

Forty-five-year-old Dr Robert Johnson, a six-foot-three black gentleman from London, was divorced and had custody of his five children, and now wanted a new partner. He had tried the personal columns and local dating agencies with little success.

Then he fell in love with the idea of taking a Russian woman for a bride.

Now this takes some swallowing, but Robert made this decision after watching Anna Kournikova on the tennis courts at Wimbledon. He was thoroughly smitten and seduced by the glamour of romancing in this way, and in this respect he was not alone, for at any one time at least eight million Western males are seeking a foreign bride. In 2001, it was estimated that these punters lost $2.5 million. Today, the figure has rocketed to over $5.8 million and the figure is still climbing.

Unfortunately, we were unable to thoroughly access Robert Johnson's outgoing emails because the British Police would have none of it. However, from police sources and one of his friends, we did obtain enough of the emails from the dating agency the doctor became involved with to enable us to piece together much of what took place during the period leading up to his disappearance.

He is now presumed dead – murdered!

Robert told a colleague, 'They're [Russian women] easier to talk to, they have degrees, they seem to be cheaper than Western women, they're easier to get on with and they don't ask for too much.'

In making this quite erroneous, somewhat bigoted assumption, Robert, who had been surfing the net for some time, obviously hadn't done his homework. Nevertheless, in October 2001, he met a young woman who called herself 'Anastasia Ustinova', a 19-year-old posing as a teacher from Omsk, Siberia. The two swapped emails and she sent him seductive photographs of herself wearing a blue micro dress and white high heels.

Robert flipped and must have completed several cartwheels. Had he known better, he would have realised that a teacher working in Siberia would be lucky to clear $50 dollars a month, $30 being nearer the mark. However, within a few weeks he would end up sending 'Anastasia' the equivalent of six or more years' wages for an average Russian.

'Anastasia has written back and said she loved me and wants to get to know me,' he told a friend. In reality, all she wanted was his money and Robert sent her plenty of her favourite commodity to pay for generous living expenses. He also bought her a diamond ring and a gold watch. The sums involved totalled around $3,250, and that was to just to start with.

We know that, on Wednesday, 17 October 2001, Robert emailed Anastasia Ustinova and two days later she replied. On Friday, 2 November, she asked for $250 for a visa, which he duly sent by Western Union Transfer.

On Tuesday, 13 November, Anastasia sent an email through the Paradise of Angels marriage agency asking for $1,050 for the air ticket and for a passport, and an extra $300 for her to use while she travelled to London. The passport money apparently went astray – although it was sent at the same time as the $1,050 – so she asked for a further $100, which he sent on 14 November. Mysteriously, the missing money was later cashed at Western Union. Robert was losing money fast.

On 23 November, his blonde bombshell wrote claiming that she had been taken ill with liver problems, so he sent her $50 for her to buy perfume.

Five days later, she wrote to say that she had stopped working because of her poor health. She claimed she had hepatitis C and that her mother and father were nursing her.

The New Year brought little respite for the eager Robert. She wanted money for a new mobile phone and cash for credit so she could text him. Her father died suddenly – in a subsequent SMS this was changed to her father-in-law.

On 2 January 2002, Robert wired Anastasia $60 for her medical care.

A week later, he sent her two Western Union transfers totalling $135. Despite this generosity, that very same day she had the temerity to ask for $250 – at least four months' wages for her – to buy sandals as she was soon to leave hospital.

All the money was sent via Western Union to Anastasia Ustinova, at Gazetnyi, Pereulok 6, Russia, who promptly collected the cash. She took a small percentage for herself, and wired the balance to two of her friends, who were sometimes known as Tatiana Ovdina, Tatyana Perlotva, Angelika, Anna Chuprakova, Elena Artemieva Yalena, Katya, Irina Taralanova, Oksana Stolyrenko and Olen Slepova – all residents of Ekaterinburg.

On 26 January, with enough money in their pockets to be able to support themselves for several years, Anastasia and her pals hit Robert Johnson again, this time for $200 for therapy. Then, on 4 March, she went the full Monty by explaining that she was going back into hospital for another operation and even more therapy, which would cost $2,000 plus $50 a day until she was discharged.

Robert was now beside himself with anxiety. He informed Anastasia of his intentions to visit her and help her out. After a few days' silence, during which she no doubt sought advice from her dating agency, she explained to him that he should only bring new US dollars, as credit card facilities were very limited – and this much was true. Fatefully, he told her that he would bring all the required funds and that he would soon be at her bedside.

Asking a friend to look after his children, he remarked, 'I feel stupid. It's like being robbed. But you have seen her picture, she is a beautiful girl. She needs me, and I need to help her out. I am in love.'

Robert then obtained a 30-day tourist visa, numbered TY

2987847, and on 21 March, after confirming his itinerary with Anastasia, he took the 10.30pm Aeroflot A310 Airbus flight from London Heathrow to Moscow, arriving at 5.20am local time. He had booked a return flight to Omsk through Thomas Cook and the passenger manifest shows that he sat in seat C39. On touchdown at Moscow, he passed through immigration control, caught the free shuttle bus and boarded his connecting flight at the internal airport, Sheremetyevo 1 (SVO 1).

Thereafter, Robert, carrying around $7,000 in new dollar bills and probably the only black man in Siberia, simply vanished.

Of course, for Robert Johnson and his children, this was a terrible tragedy, but at this remove it is probably instructive to remind ourselves of the sums involved. All in all, this single scam netted the dating agency around $11,000, which is the staggering, if not obscene, equivalent of 25 years' wages to the average Russian. In the West, this equates to about $500,000.

Every year, tens of thousands of Western men travel to Eastern Europe and the Far East in search of true love. They are well catered for because more than a thousand sites advertise their brochures, videos and the 'entertainment' events they organise. The phenomenon amply demonstrates how sex-tour companies and certain marriage agencies contribute to the exploitation and objectification of women and women's bodies by promoting prostitution and pornography.

A few moments ago, we gently questioned the sanity of some of the men who go seeking love on the internet. But, of course, we have done their homework, and when you read the following you may come to the conclusion that men can be even dumber that we initially thought.

One genuine agency did furnish us with correspondence from

several male clients, and as we read the letters to a totally honest woman from her prospective suitors we could see how fortunate she was not to pick any of them.

Doctors, surgeons, engineers, property developers, all queued up alongside religious fruit cakes, college dropouts and the lost and the lonely to court this girl. Several of these humanoids had 'I am mentally unstable and capable of mass murder' written all over their faces and throughout the text of their letters, one of which bore an uncanny resemblance to the scribbling hand of the serial killer William Heirens, who issued the challenge 'Catch Me Before I Kill Again'.

Yet, strange to relate, interspersed among these desperate refugees from Bedlam, this assortment of knuckle-dragging, body-pierced primates, were a few honest, well-motivated men who were sincerely seeking love. Nevertheless, we were amused to see that one guy was generous enough to send the lady a dollar bill and a scrap of lined paper torn from a notebook, to help her reply to him.

This man, from Los Angeles, claimed he was a high-powered engineer, yet his grammar and command of the English language said otherwise, being among the worst we have ever seen. His photo, as he stared at the camera, revealed the face of the type of hoodlum commonly seen in Mafia movies garrotting someone in the back seat of a large, black car. That this man hoped to win the heart of any discerning woman was sad.

Another of our favourite letters was a handwritten note extolling the sender's own virtues and pledging his undying love for the recipient. He added, enthusiastically but barely legibly, this unforgettable advice: 'DO NOT TRUST ANYONE YOU MEET

OVER THE INTERNET. NEVER MEET ANYONE ON RAILWAY STATIONS OR IN BARS. THEY MAY RAPE AND KILL YOU.'

Surprisingly, he didn't follow this sanguine warning with an invitation to meet him under the clock by platform eight.

Of course, there were scores of letters from thoroughly decent guys. All well written and very polite, and it was clear that every one of these men was genuinely besotted with the girl. However, letters like these were outnumbered by those from out-and-out fantasists, many bordering on the lunatic fringe.

A splendid example was a typed letter from a man old enough to be her grandfather. Overweight and bespectacled, he claimed to have the strength and physique of a 20-year-old. 'I follow a military exercise regime for elite soldiers,' he wrote.

Here, we thought, was God's gift to all women. And a pillar of rectitude: he didn't smoke and not a drop of alcohol had ever passed his lips. He also boasted that he lived on Hawaii, an earthly paradise. To back up this wild assertion, he sent a postcard of some beautiful Hawaiian scenery, adding that his house would have been clearly visible were it not for the fact that it was hidden just behind the clump of lush, green trees in the distance. On top of that, his CV read like that of a candidate shortlisted for the job of Pope.

This model of all the virtues then demonstrated that he was a gifted diplomat by asking his prospective paramour, 'How is your economic situation?' Oblivious to the intrusive nature of his enquiry, he further demolished his credibility by asking baldly, 'Do you have any mental or physical diseases or problems? Do you smoke, drink, or use drugs?'

What woman wouldn't melt under such a charm offensive?

At this point, we had intended to move on but before we do

we can't resist unburdening ourselves of just one more of these lovelorn suitors.

A man of exemplary humility and modesty, 'Mike' told this lass he had spent over a year searching the internet for the perfect wife. 'I have looked at several thousand pictures and read all the biographies,' he said, adding, 'I have researched and sorted until I have narrowed my choices down to nine women of which you are one that I am writing to.'

A *mere* nine women! *Wasn't* she a lucky girl! We are talking Russian *Playboy* centrefold material, a woman fluent in four languages and studying her fifth, Japanese, who wakes one morning to find that Dame Fortune has plucked her from obscurity and made her one of nine women that Mike has chosen as a possible candidate for a wife. She would be walking on air. No doubt he would, generously, sleep with each in turn to aid him with his selection.

Several months later, the thoughtful Mike sent her a second, identical letter, apparently having forgotten the content of his first one. Despite his clumsiness, it was the audacity of the man that appealed to us.

For this we give him credit. No, we will award him first prize!

After all, Mike was, in his own words, 'a quite famous French chef'. A man who 'became tired of cooking fine food in the classic manner for people who could not taste the difference…' 'Romantic and very much an old Knight or gentleman' was his self-effacing description of himself. This man ignorantly assumes Russian women are so naive and stupid that they cannot read between the lines.

Any man who is keen to meet a Russian bride might be interested to learn that one of the Soviet Union's greatest achievements is education. From being an agrarian society in which literacy was limited to the few in the upper classes, the Russian Federation has developed to achieve a literacy rate of 98 per cent, among the best in the world, and truancy is unknown. Modern Russian women are a damn sight brighter than the three Western clowns featured above.

MONA JAUD AWANA: CYBER TERRORIST

The outrage caused by the murder of a young Israeli at the hands of a bloodthirsty Palestinian terrorist group was all the more shocking because the internet had facilitated the killing. For obvious reasons in these troubled times, the manufactured 'romantic' chatroom contact that evolved between a Palestinian and an Israeli is not a commonplace occurrence. So, when it became clear that a young Jewish lad had been cruelly tricked by a duplicitous Palestinian girl and viciously slain by her accomplices, the immediate reaction was one of overwhelming anger.

Incensed exchanges flew across the internet – the very vehicle that had spawned this tragic event – with sites and weblogs springing up to passionately rail against perceived injustices, rekindling dormant hatreds.

One bitter posting suggested that this salutary case should be required reading within the Israeli school system, and went on to proclaim, 'For while Ofir had "Sleeping With the Enemy" (another American movie!) on his mind, Mona was out for blood… HIS blood!'

Anger and resentment abounded, old wounds were reopened and exacerbated – and the internet was a major tool in it all.

Mona Jaud Awana lived in the small West Bank Arab village of Bir Naballah, just a few miles north of Jerusalem and a short distance south of Ramallah.

Down the ages, Ramallah has seen much bloodshed, and 23-year-old Awana had a plan that promised more of the same: the abduction of a young Jewish man whom she would later cast into the jaws of death.

Awana's first step was to find a sure way of achieving her sinister purpose, and she turned immediately to the internet for assistance.

In an internet cafe in Ramallah, Awana cast her lure. She was not just someone planning a terrible crime; in fact, she was a spoke in a more ruthless wheel, for she was a diehard member of the student wing of Al Fatah's Tanzim terror organisation.

Awana's plan was endorsed by those around her. She would be charged with drawing a young Jew into her spider's web, and they would then dispatch the trusting victim.

Awana had the perfect lure – sex.

Her first contact was established with a young man from Jerusalem named Meir Karni. Awana delved into an internet chatroom to find him, and quickly set about promising him sex if he would care to visit her in Ramallah.

As a young, red-blooded male, Meir was intrigued, indeed tantalised, by some of the lewd suggestions Awana put his way, but fortunately for him his savvy prevailed and he declined the offer. There was something about the urgency of Awana's approach that had made him wary. She seemed just a little *too* keen to get him to Ramallah.

Undeterred, Awana adopted the online pseudonym of 'Sally' and, after a short period of trawling, hooked herself another young Jew, Ofir Rahum. Sally's fabricated background led the 16-year-old to believe that her father was of Moroccan descent, her mother Israeli, and that she herself was an immigrant from Morocco, not yet proficient in Hebrew. She let Ofir know that she had not long been resident in Ramallah. To Awana's delight, the teenager seemed interested. She rushed back to her accomplices to report that her target wanted more. For his part, Ofir entertained his friends with his tale of meeting an older, alluring woman on the internet.

Along with the many messages he sent via the net, Ofir had emailed Sally a photograph of himself. He looked and sounded exactly what he was: a handsome and intelligent youth. Sadly, even the brightest of individuals, if lonely or desperate enough, sometimes throw caution to the wind. Even so, how could Ofir have fallen for someone he had never even met and really knew nothing about?

The answer is, it happens all the time. Just ask anybody you know who engages in – and may even be hopelessly addicted to – internet flirting, whether through emails, postings on discussion boards or in private chatrooms. The young and adventurous especially, believing – because they *want* to – that their lucky number has come up, will take the most outrageous of risks.

Meanwhile, the Tanzim posse were thrilled, and instructed their friend Mona to keep a firm grip on this most recent contact. She must tempt him and tease him as much as possible, as a prelude to enticing him to meet her.

After a number of online chatroom sessions, Awana had decided that Ofir was a suitable candidate. She duly passed this information to a pal, one of those pulling her jaded strings: a brutal terrorist named Hassan al-Qadi.

Blissfully unaware of the danger he was in, Ofir let his mind be filled with images of the seductive 'Sally'. Over a couple of weeks, Awana worked hard to lure him to what she called a 'one-on-one' encounter at a Jerusalem apartment belonging to one of her girlfriends. However, Ofir told her this would not be convenient for him. He explained he couldn't travel to Jerusalem, enjoy the proposed steamy interlude, then get back to Ashkelon without his parents becoming suspicious about the length of time he would be away from home.

Realising that her target would not be swayed, Awana backed off for the moment.

Later that month, Awana finally succeeded in snaring her prey. On Wednesday, 17 January 2001, the two arranged to meet at the central bus station in Jerusalem. Ofir had been asked to bring a large sum of money with him, and was very excited about the sexual encounter that was surely to follow.

When the two met, he eagerly agreed to accompany Awana, by taxi, to the A-Ram junction, north of Jerusalem. It was here that Hassan al-Qadi had said he would leave a car for Awana.

After finding the vehicle, Awana drove off with Ofir towards Ramallah. The teenager would have been acutely aware, along with the rest of this troubled land, that two Israeli reservists had been seized and slaughtered in the town just a few months back, in October 2000. The pair had been savagely beaten, tossed from a window and torn apart by a baying crowd thirsty for their blood.

But did Ofir Rahum sense that a terrible trap might lie in wait for him too?

Awana pulled over to the side of the road when they got to El Bireh, not far from the village of Psigot.

The ambush happened just as they had planned it. Awana leaped out of the car and al-Qadi, accompanied by two masked Palestinian hit-team members, suddenly appeared at the passenger door. Yanking it open and shoving a Kalashnikov AK-47 into the terrified lad's face, al-Qadi screamed at him to get out. Panicked, Ofir remained seated, shaking his head wildly.

At this unexpected defiance – the group had obviously thought that fear would render their captive more compliant, so that they could take him away, presumably to extend his suffering – al-Qadi reacted with extreme violence. Enraged, he fired several shots into Ofir's legs, then attempted to drag him from the car. Still resisting his attacker, the teenager received a hail of bullets in his face and upper torso.

Ofir Rahum, expecting an enjoyable experience with an attractive woman, instead ended up shot dead by a band of terrorists. His once trusted and familiar internet had betrayed him with lethal consequences.

Awana climbed back into the car and followed the others as they sped away, leaving one of their number to dispose of Ofir. The youth's corpse, riddled with 15 bullets, was driven a short distance before being unceremoniously dumped at the dusty roadside.

Shortly after the slaying, Awana met a girlfriend for lunch, visited an aunt in the hospital, then attended a defensive driving course in Jerusalem. It was business as usual for the cold-blooded internet siren.

The anxious parents of Ofir Rahum, concerned when he failed to return home, questioned his friends, soon discovering that he had not attended school that day. His body was discovered that same evening, but was unrecognisable and presumed to be that of a Palestinian collaborator dispatched by a bunch of vigilantes.

Palestinian security officials laid claim to the victim's remains. However, because of the extreme mutilation of the victim's features by gunshot wounds, investigators had difficulty identifying the body. Later, the vigilante theory now dropped, they suggested it was that of a Palestinian, apparently shot dead by Israeli security officials. Israel vehemently denied this, and noted that shots had been fired at an army convoy in the area of El Bireh.

The bickering continued, with the Israelis arguing that it was the Palestinians who were responsible for the murder.

The Palestinians continued to advertise the fact that they had discovered a body, but declined to offer a description or any other information. When the Civil Administration in Judaea and Samaria and the Israeli Defence Forces (IDF) received a report on the missing boy, Israel once again pressed for details. The Palestinians stuck to their claim that they held a body of one of their own. Not to be discouraged by this, senior Israeli officials supplied them with a full description of Ofir Rahum and other important details, demanding immediate co-operation.

Under mounting pressure, Palestinian security officials soon confirmed Israel's suspicions and Ofir's body was handed over to the District Coordinating Office in Ramallah.

'We take this kind of murder very seriously, since it is harmful to the PA,' stated a Palestinian security officer. He also commented that both nationalistic and criminal motives were being investigated.

Despite the continuing Israeli–Palestinian conflict, WAFA, a news agency controlled by the Palestinian Authority, denounced the murder of Ofir Rahum, stating that it fully opposed attacks against civilians. Israel's Prime Minister, Ehud Barak, also condemned the killing, saying, 'The cruel murder of a young man is extremely grave and we will act to ensure those responsible are brought to justice.'

Ofir Rahum was the fourth Israeli to be murdered in the Ramallah area since the outbreak of the latest intifada.

The invulnerability Mona Jaud Awana assumed she enjoyed by using the internet under a false name did not last long. She was arrested a few weeks after the killing by Israeli agents and an undercover army unit at the home of her parents in the village of Bir Naballah. An examination of Ofir Rahum's computer had led the authorities straight there.

It emerged that Awana was a freelance journalist and resident of East Jerusalem who carried an Israeli identity card. Palestinian sources in Ramallah quickly let it be known that it was highly unlikely that this former psychology student at Bir Zeit University was involved in the murder. And at first Awana refused to help the police. 'Despite the fact that she has been detained for many hours, she is not co-operating at this stage and we still don't have all the details,' said Israel Police Inspector General Shlomo Aharonishky. 'She is denying her involvement. We still don't have the motive or what lay behind the deed, but the investigation is still going on.' But, he added, 'from evidence collected at her home and elsewhere, we believe she is connected to it'.

The Al Fatah activists to whom Awana was closely affiliated also distanced themselves from the murder. And her brother said she did not have a computer at home and was not familiar with the workings of the internet. A spurious allegation indeed, as Awana is known to have made regular visits to internet cafes and ably navigated her way around the web.

Mona Jaud Awana was charged with Ofir Rahum's murder, which she subsequently admitted playing her part in, and brought before the Beit El Military Court, near Ramallah. Without one shred of remorse, she proudly announced that the murder had been committed on behalf of 'the Palestinian people'.

And, while Prime Minister Barak was busy praising the IDF and General Security Service for the efficient operation that had led to Awana's arrest, he took the opportunity to warn that Israel would apprehend and severely punish those others who had a hand in Ofir's slaughter.

As Awana's trial loomed, many furious Israelis expressed their fears that a gaggle of eager left-wing Jewish lawyers would clamour to represent the notorious defendant.

In November 2002, a Zionist military court passed a life sentence on Mona Jaud Awana for participation in the kidnap and murder of a Zionist settler, Ofir Rahum. The court found Mona guilty of 'intentionally causing the death of a man', which, in the Zionist penal code, is a crime tantamount to first-degree murder.

The body of Ofir Rahum was later returned to his parents so that they could bury their son. Candle-lit vigils were also held in remembrance of this young man, conned out of his life by a group of predators. Emotions ran high, especially after it was made public that the murdered teenager was initially thought to have been a Palestinian collaborator.

Hundreds attended Ofir's funeral in Ashkelon. His school principal described him as 'an outstanding student and a wonderful person, who had been blessed with the support of a loving family'.

In the wake of the Rahum's slaying, Chief-Superintendent Meir Zohar, head of the Israel Police Computer Crime Department, announced that internet-related crime was on the increase. He stated that the tragedy was the first instance that he knew of in which the internet had been used specifically to entrap a targeted terrorist victim.

'The criminal underworld realised the potential of the internet a long time ago,' Zohar said. 'It allows criminals to masquerade as different people and provides them with a large degree of anonymity.'

As well as all the familiar crimes that the internet provides a haven for, such as hacking, gambling, drug-smuggling, rape and paedophilia, young people were often the perpetrators of cyber crimes, he explained, and those juveniles needed to be made fully aware of the consequences of their actions. 'I think what is needed is a policy of education and information to make internet users, especially minors, more aware of the risk they are taking,' he said.

On the anniversary of the Computer Crimes Department, which often keeps tabs on chatroom conversations, Zohar claimed that this electronic eavesdropping had been particularly effective on two previous occasions. The first had been when police had monitored discussions between several people threatening to commit suicide. Investigators established contact and provided them with the necessary treatment.

The other case involved a chatroom participant who claimed that she was a victim of incestuous abuse. Police immediately opened an investigation into her allegations.

Shula Rahum, Ofir's mother, observed, 'Maybe parents should warn their kids about computers like they do with drugs and diseases. They should browse through their chats to see whom they are communicating with and where they are going.'

Ofir's parents had no idea what he had been doing, nor who had so skilfully seduced him via his computer. Shalom Rahum says that he only found out afterwards, from his son's school friends, and that was far too late.

SATOMI MITARAI: SURFED TO DESTRUCTION

'So you're saying that every anti-social 11-year-old is going to kill someone? Or are you insinuating that every anti-social person is going to go on a killing rampage? I'm anti-social but I'm not gonna go around killing people. Though sometimes it'd be nice...'

INTERNET CHATROOM USER ON THE JAPANESE SCHOOLGIRL KILLER CASE

On June 2001, the watching world recoiled as news of a former caretaker at Ikeda Elementary School, in a suburb of Osaka, 250 miles west of Tokyo, went berserk and stormed the building armed with a kitchen knife.

The 39-year-old, who had a long history of mental illness, rampaged through the schoolyard and classrooms, slashing away at as many children as he could lay his hands on. He had managed to stab eight of them to death before he was brought to ground.

The judge presiding over the trial of Mamoru Takuma at Osaka District Court wasted little time in sentencing him to death by hanging, choosing to reject his defence of insanity and instead finding him entirely culpable of committing the murders of seven girls and a boy aged between six and eight, who had cowered in their classrooms during his onslaught.

Takuma had also attacked a number of other people that fateful day, injuring 13 small children and two teachers. The judge had no qualms about sentencing this man to death, just as Takuma himself had felt no compunction about massacring his way through Ikeda Elementary School. The convicted killer had even informed the court that he would have killed more had he had the forethought to carry out his spree at a local kindergarten.

Without any obvious displays of remorse, Takuma, who suffered from a long-term schizophrenic condition, was hauled out of the public eye by guards, to await his fate. Japan was faced yet again with the fallout from another example of extreme violence in its school system.

Tuesday, 1 June 2004 saw the emergence of another terrifying attack on a young person at her school, only this time, rather than some deranged, socially inadequate adult, her killer was one of her peers, both girls having attended Sasebo Elementary School in Nagasaki Prefecture.

That day, an 11-year-old girl calmly approached her classmate, pretty 12-year-old Satomi Mitarai, and unleashed an explosion of violence against her with a knife. Her throat and arms slashed, Satomi slumped to the floor, instantly losing consciousness from massive loss of blood. She died later that day.

Her killer, for legal reasons known only as 'Girl A' but later dubbed 'Nevada' on the internet, left her to die, returning to her classroom covered in her victim's blood, to greet her shocked teacher and fellow pupils.

Unsurprisingly, the story made the headlines around the world, for nobody could comprehend how this child had reached the point where she was able to methodically butcher a school friend in broad daylight. It came as a huge shock, this grisly homicide, the like of which could have been seen in any number of gory 'slasher' movies. In fact, this young female killer had quite a predilection for such dubious entertainment. This fascination was just one of the factors that led her to act on the appalling fantasies she had developed, most of which revolved around killing.

At her trial, Nevada was quickly sentenced and placed in a juvenile facility where, it is said, she will languish until at least 2013.

The ghastly nature of her crime, and the constant media notoriety it generated, marred the psyches of those around her, perhaps for ever. However, her story did not end with her incarceration. Rather, her actions that June day would spawn an internet phenomenon – dark, perverse, but not altogether impossible to understand, given today's often murky online climate.

Tucked within the recesses of the vast Japanese realm of the web, a photograph depicting a school class was posted. Two of the girls in the picture are instantly identifiable.

On the far left stands a young girl, grinning broadly, wearing spectacles and a green sweatshirt. It is Satomi Mitarai, and the obviously delighted child presents to the camera a triumphant finger-sign of victory.

Beside Satomi is another girl, lacking all the joy and vitality of her glossy-haired classmate. This girl has a strange, unreadable expression on her face. Like a spirit in a ghostly portrait, a dark harbinger of things to come, this child would one day be Satomi's executioner.

The enduring image of an outwardly normal-looking pre-teen, clutching a box-cutting knife and with murder in her heart, has scored a deep groove in the communal consciousness of the internet. Stories detailing Nevada's crime were later posted on online forums across Europe, the United States and Asia. Especially in Japan, with its steady undercurrent of horror movies and its creation of extremely graphic and often sexually violent cartoon imagery, where this kind of killer culture is keenly embraced, Nevada became an instant focus of attention.

Indeed, an online cartoon character would be based upon her. It did not take long for this juvenile murderer to be assigned the moniker of 'Nevada-tan'; the 'tan' suffix presumably used to connote a child's pronunciation of the honorific '-chan'.

The police investigation into the shocking murder of Satomi Mitarai and the background of her young slayer revealed that Nevada was, at least initially, a relatively normal child, with no overt history of bad behaviour, let alone a propensity for violence. It was noted that she had a keen interest in horror films and any other form of entertainment featuring murder and mayhem, from TV shows to comic books.

A particular favourite of hers is the Japanese cult film *Battle Royale.* Made by Kinjt Fukasaku in 2000, it is the story of a group of young students who are taken to a tiny, remote island and handed a map, food and various weapons, then made to hunt and kill each other in ways that would have had the schoolboys of *The Lord of the Flies* running for cover. The film, exceptionally popular the world over, was consumed voraciously by the impressionable Nevada.

Another of her favourite movies was *Voice*. This charts the descent of a girl who goes insane and embarks upon a savage killing spree. Though Nevada enjoyed a diet of violent films like these at the time, it seems that she had an outlet in the form of basketball. However, after being forced out of her team, at the behest of her mother, to focus on improving her school results, Nevada chose to retreat further into her fantasy world of death, becoming surly with her parents and those around her.

By now, the lure of the internet had started to overtake all else. She began collecting 'flash' horror movies on a website she had started, and would frequent many violent sites, constantly searching for more bloody fodder. She would regularly access a site, viewed by these authors, that features a short story entitled *The Red Room*, in which a boy is slashed to death. There is a warning on the opening page advising that those with a 'weak heart' should steer clear.

Concentrating as much of her time as she could on the internet, and regarding the real world as superfluous, she aimed to induce other web visitors to join her site and share in her domain by commencing her own blog – an online live diary – detailing her interests, and even regaling those that came to see with gruesome stories and cooking recipes.

The following extract appeared on the website – now removed – run by Nevada:

Birthday	21 November 1992
Blood type	A [in Japan, blood type is said to determine fate, like a horoscope]
Hobbies	Watching movies
Favourite animal	Cat
Favourite sport	Basketball
Favourite music	[no answer given]
What do you treasure?	That's a se*cr*et!

Also worthy of note is her interest in the TV horror series *Monday Mystery Theatre*, in which a number of unfortunate victims are brutally dispatched with box-cutters. Nevada later threatened a boy with such a tool, and ten days after the incident led Satomi Mitarai into an empty classroom, covered her eyes and slit the girl's throat with one.

Nevada and Satomi Mitarai had been close friends. They were in an art class together, played basketball together, shared a group diary and often passed notes on an internet 'home page' bulletin board. But Nevada turned into a mortal enemy after Satomi made the gross error of slighting her about her physical appearance, using her online journal to do so.

Nevada demanded an apology for what she perceived as an insult, the worse for coming from someone she considered a friend. Satomi refused, instead branding her 'pretentious'. The final straw came when Mitarai typed another message commenting on Nevada's weight. This marked her out for death. The message was posted four days before she was murdered.

On the day of the killing, the girls' teacher said she first noticed something unusual when the two had been missing from class. But, before a search for them was begun, Nevada returned, her hands and clothing spattered with Satomi Mitarai's blood. After the police were called, Nevada confessed to the murder, sobbing, 'I have done a bad thing.'

She later explained under police questioning that her relationship with her friend had curdled after the hurtful and humiliating remarks Satomi, the more attractive girl, had made about her during exchanges in internet chatrooms.

Inevitably, the Japanese media later highlighted the dangers of this form of interpersonal communication. Similar to text messaging, this method of conversing with another person does not easily convey nuances or subtleties. Neither can it give a precise indication of their mood. As a result, intentions can be misread and animosity can burgeon when one person misconstrues the intention of another participant.

Describing the event that day to police, Nevada stated, 'She [Mitarai] wrote something bad about my appearance several times on the net a few days before the incident. I didn't like that, so I called her [to a classroom] and slashed her neck after getting her to sit on a chair.'

Revealing that the murder had been premeditated, she took investigators through the planning and preparation she had made. She told how she had been inspired to use the small knife after seeing the method used in one of her favoured television shows. 'I saw that drama,' she stated. 'I thought I'd do it that way.'

In the aftermath of the killing, Nevada had expressed remorse, going so far as to openly question her inexplicable actions. 'I wonder why I did it. If I thought and acted properly, it wouldn't have happened. I would like to apologise.'

A psychiatric examination found her to be suffering from no effects of any recognised mental disorder. Nevertheless, the sudden outward alteration in Nevada's behaviour sparked concerns that the problem may be broader. Once again, the internet became the prime target. 'Over a computer… you can't see the person's face, so it's easier to use increasingly violent language. If that's the case, it's an incident that reflects a pathology of society in the age of the internet,' declared the *Tokyo Shimbun*, a major metropolitan newspaper.

Around this time, other national papers covered stories about the surging use of the internet by children, reporting, courtesy of the Telecommunications Ministry, that 62 per cent of Japanese children between the ages of six and 12 have internet access. The gruesome crime committed by Nevada cast a pall over the emphasis on technology, which is particularly marked within the country's schools.

'What children need most is to be able to piece together real things and real experiences,' wrote Hisashi Sonoda, an internet crime expert at Konan University.

'We must make children understand even more the basic importance of life,' the newspaper *Yomiuri* said in an editorial.

Although Japan is still reportedly one of the safest of all the developed nations, youth crime has dramatically increased there in recent years. In fact, the number of children under 14 committing serious crimes in 2003 rose to 212, an increase on the previous year of 47 per cent.

Youth crime in Japan has been a source of great concern since a horrific incident dating from 1997, in which a 14-year-old lad murdered an 11-year-old, placing the boy's severed head outside the gates of the school the two attended.

This shocking incident nudged Japan's parliament a step in the right direction: it lowered the age of criminal responsibility from 16 to 14.

In 2002, a 12-year-old boy in Nagasaki was accused of the murder of a toddler by pushing him from a rooftop.

Nevada, too young to be punished under Japan's penal code, was transferred to juvenile detention until her case was determined in a family court.

This horrific crime, perpetrated by one so young, stirred up as much sensation as might be expected, especially in media-frenzied Japan. It is another example of internet addiction leading to destruction: in this case, not just one life, but two. And not only did the lure of the net drag Nevada away from what she should have been focusing on in her real, everyday life and feed her horror-orientated interests to dangerous proportions: but, bizarrely, it also helped to turn her into a celebrity in the wake of her atrocity.

Many began to cruise the internet looking for the latest piece of 'fan art' to do with young Nevada, or sought to join the most recent chatroom discussion about her. This tragic, lonely, 11-year-old killer was transformed into an online phenomenon – perhaps as bold a statement about the perverse pull of the internet as one can make.

MEN AND WOMEN BEHIND BARS: INTERNET LOVEBIRDS

In 2001, something extremely strange started happening at the Super-Max Correctional Facility at Broward, where the state of Florida also houses its female Death Row population. Indeed, the events unfolding at the Florida Department of Corrections' (FDC) headquarters led to worn-out soles and bald patches in the plush carpet of the director's office, after one its most unattractive inmates started to receive a lot of mail.

At first, the letters arrived in a trickle, which then became a flood, before growing, to the consternation and alarm of officials, into a daily tidal wave of packages of all sizes and from all around the world.

At first, the prison's censors – already overworked and underpaid at the best of times – vetted the contents but soon a collective 'Fuck this!' went around the mail room. People started scratching their heads because *every single letter* professed undying love for inmate FDC # 160885 Robin J Lunceford. Moreover, most of the registered mail contained cheques, money orders and cash in amounts ranging from $50 to several thousand.

Diners in the prison officers' canteen screamed in unison, 'Beeeeee Jeeeeezus' after one donation of $8,000 dropped on the mat for Robin Lunceford.

With no fewer than three aliases, and more tattoos than a fairground worker, this ungodly-looking felon had committed more robberies using a firearm than Bonnie and Clyde, and has drawn a staggering 260 years' punishment for her crimes. So why all the fan mail?

By the time Ms Lunceford's prison bank account reached $1.8 million, the combined intelligence of the Florida Department of Corrections was at its wit's end, yet the money continued to roll in. She agreed to receive only a few female visitors and a shrewd little attorney; she wasn't replying to much of the mail and, as far as the prison authorities could see, she wasn't running an illegal business from jail.

It is a popular misconception that scamming originated in Eastern Europe. As we mentioned in our first chapter, it started in America with Peters and Takers, and maybe this had now returned to haunt them. However, Lunceford's fiddle put her predecessors in the shade. She became, and still is, the Einstein of Scam.

Early in 2002, a colleague of one of the authors at the Criminology Research Institute rushed into work clasping a note on which was written: 'Women Behind Bars'. It referred to an internet-run dating agency dedicated solely to American prisoners seeking love. We checked out WBB's website and on one of the pages saw a photo of one of the most beautiful women on the planet.

Clad in French red underwear, black stockings and stiletto shoes, this creature was as hot as chilli peppers.

Robin's profile gave few other details – notably absent was her rich criminal CV – but she alluded to her search for an older, financially stable man, and possible suitors were invited to write to the dating agency and pay around $17 for her address.

Smelling a rat, we wired the money, and after it had cleared – it was refunded later – we received an email with Robin's address at Broward, Pembroke Pines, Florida. And at that time the lady's next-door neighbour was the serial killer Aileen Wuornos!

But then we carried out a very simple exercise. Within seconds we had logged on to the FDC's Inmate Search, typed in Robin's name and ID number, and bingo, up popped a photograph of the real Robin Lunceford that bore no resemblance at all to the sexy shot of supermodel Laetitia Casta that appeared on WBB's website.

Try doing a search for yourself and check out the FDC site, along with anything you can find on Laetitia. We're sure you'll notice the difference. Unfortunately, the Florida state government and its entire prison system had not.

But the $1.8 million was by no means the end of it.

We drew this discrepancy to the attention of Women Behind Bars, who politely explained that 'We do not check out photographic details' but assured us that they would do so in the future. Of course, WBB must have earned a tidy sum from this caper, and obviously they could not have noticed the striking likeness between one of the world's most famous models and the photo they had posted on their site.

We also contacted the Florida Department of Law Enforcement, based in Tallahassee. It soon became clear that Robin Lunceford really had polished up her scheme. She had handed all of her mail to her few visitors – all quite legal – and they had replied to the potential suitors with a duplicated series of correspondence – all carefully worded and sending a message to this effect: 'I don't have much time to write because I study a lot. I am working for university degrees in economics and teaching. You are so handsome and kind. I could fall for you. Here are some more of my pictures. I hope you like them because they are just for you, etc. I have my own website, which will show I am innocent. Please write to my mother on the physical address there.'

Now short-circuiting the prison system, the excited suitors logged on to a porn site containing carefully doctored photos. 'I used to be a model,' it was claimed on the first page. 'I trusted a man and he got me in trouble with the Law.'

Writing to the 'mother' drew the standard response: '…not many men write me because they are afraid of my beauty. My heart is warm and I would love to walk and dine with you by a fire… etc… if you can help me with a little money, I know you are sincerely in love with me… etc.'

Thousands of mugs from around the world did exactly that. They sent more money… serious money. Of course, when any punter asked if he could visit Robin, he received another standard reply, one that rounded things off nicely: 'Darling, I would adore seeing you – perhaps for a few minutes alone. I ache for you, darling. I am so happy. When I passed your letter to the prison governor, she said no. It was against the rules. If you write to them, they will punish me. It has broken my heart.'

The fact of the matter is, Robin Lunceford is not able to receive general visitors, period, because of her security status, and the FDC does not, as a matter of policy, enter into correspondence with people who wish to do so – not least thousands of them all gagging to see the woman.

It is true to say that many of the women featured on WBB's site have a genuine intention of finding a soul mate and hope to get married and settle down once they have paid their debt to society. However, a percentage of these women not only want to fleece you of every dollar you have saved or are likely to ever earn, but are also *extremely dangerous*. Here are just a few of them:

Inmate ADC # 704072 Kimberley F Forrester

Ms Forrester, who has two aliases, is serving 50 years for offences including forgery, theft by receiving, probation violation, possession of firearms and criminal conspiracy. She used a photograph of an international model to sell herself, and Kim is no shrinking violet, for she was vociferous when it came to asking for money. When we brought this delicate matter to the attention of the Arkansas Department of Corrections and the internet agency itself, it was discovered that this evil woman had been getting away with this type of fraud for ages.

You will be pleased to learn, however, that her parole expectations have since been drastically reduced after the authors contacted the prison.

Inmate KDOC # 55885/004966 Rebecca Kincer

But there are good stories to be had, so it is not all bad news. Dick, 69, from the USA, first saw convicted murderess 62-year-old Rebecca 'Becky' Kincer on the WBB website in February

1999. He wrote to her on St Valentine's Day 'as a lark', he said in an email to the authors.

'She just hit me as a fun person and I wrote back,' he told us. 'I received an answer much quicker than I expected and we started writing daily. It wasn't long before we started fighting via mail because I thought she wanted money, but it was because something I had written was misinterpreted.'

However, ever pleased to bring you some good and exciting news, we are delighted to report that the couple are now blissfully married and the white-haired lady in question will be released in 2040.

Dick said, 'She will either come home to me or I will die here waiting for her! She is my life and I will never leave her.'

Inmate MDC # 167734 Carmel Cynthia Robinson

Philip A Robinson hit a three-cherry jackpot after contacting a woman who advertised on the WBB site. After a rollercoaster ride of a relationship, including the shredding of one of her letters after she threatened to break with him, they were married on 26 June 2001, in the Visitors Room of the Scotts Correctional Facility in Plymouth, Michigan.

However, unknown to Phillip, he had been kept in the dark.

Born on 5 September 1961, Carmel has several aliases: Carmel Allen, Cynthia Moss, Cynthia Reed, Sharon Green and Shirley Hall. Her crimes are: assault to commit murder (30 years); manslaughter (ten years); carrying concealed weapons (six months); escape from prison (six months); uttering and publishing (two and a half years).

The couple's present marital status is unknown.

Mr Lenny Madrid, however, had a less than loving relationship when he met a lady through WBB's site. He wrote to complain to the agency on 13 August 2001:

'The relationship I had with one of your ladies from your listing was a joke. She provided me with a photo that was not what it seemed to be. She had consistently requested me to send money, but, as long as I didn't get a recent photo of her, her cash flow became smaller. Upon her release, she waited two weeks before she told me they let her out. Anyway, she was a conniver to get me to send money. The last amount she asked for was $600,000, claiming she needed to move out to a different house with her mother. She claimed that with her criminal record she was finding it hard to find a place to live. I sent her money and a phone card to call me once she got the $100 I sent her. Well, it has been a month now since we have had contact with one another. I don't plan on contacting her in any way. I figure she'll be back in the jail system before the end of the year. This relationship has come to an end, by me giving up the idea of getting married to her. Thank you for your site.'

But, not one to be thwarted, Lenny has since met another female prisoner, who said she wanted to marry him when she is released. Careful, Lenny, you should have learned a lesson or two by now!

Tommy, from the USA, rather sums it all up in his email:

'Dear Christopher, I met someone thru WBB, visited her in prison many times and thought things were wonderful and I still have the letters to prove it, and once she got the TV

> money, she now claims she never asked for the jig was up and not only did she not write, she did not let me visit her any more. Her friend does the same thing and has 15 guys on a list that she calls. I even saw someone come to visit her friend and would have warned him but I was not given the chance because of tight security. These girls are professional con artists and trade their skills around to get money to buy clothes and ice cream and whatever from unsuspecting people like me who get drawn into this by the elaborate web they weave. They are very convincing and ruin it for the few real good honest women trying to reach out for a penpal and beyond. I don't trust any of them, nor the guards any more. Women Behind Bars is ruined by the very people it serves.'

Actually, Women Behind Bars is run by two pretty decent Christian people. They have been more than fair when dealing with the authors and we are sure they will endorse the following.

The bottom line is enjoying the search for your bride-to-be, even on the sites which advertise female criminals. But remember this: they are in prison for offences ranging from fraud, through drugs and armed robbery, to murder. One of America's most vicious female killers advertised on WBB's site. And did she have some nerve!

Lora Lee Zaiontz was a co-defendant with TDC # 999784 Troy Albert Kunkle. For any girls who may have a compulsion to write to the handsome Troy, bear in mind that he was executed by lethal injection on 1 April 2005.

But, if you look up Troy's rap sheet under 'Texas Executed Offenders' before you write to Lora, at least you'll know what you are letting yourself in for.

There are hundreds of websites set up for convicted inmates who either want pen friends or are cunningly protesting their innocence in money-making schemes. Here we expose a few of them. Don't get sucked in.

RODGERS, Jeremiah (Florida # 123101) DOB 19.04.1977

'I'm positive, a good listener. I am outgoing, generous, respectful, friendly, caring and humorous.'

This is how necrophiliac Rodgers ludicrously describes himself on the internet. And this killer awaits his fate in Florida's electric chair for shooting a man in what only can be described as a 'thrill killing', in Santa Rosa County, Florida. Weighing 146 pounds, with brown eyes and brown hair, Rodgers has his birth sign, the Ram's horns, tattooed on his head.

Of the events that put him on Death Row, there isn't an enormous amount of detail on record. However, the basic facts are that Rodgers loosed off a volley of shots at a person's home and missed his intended target. He later returned, shot a man dead and committed some pretty awful sexual acts on the corpse.

The repugnant Rodgers, who advertises for pen friends on the internet, describes his eye colour as blue – they are brown – and says he enjoys reading, crosswords, playing volleyball, chess and 'learning new things'.

OSBORNE, Larry Cecil (Kentucky # 121516) DOB 22.03.1980

Nineteen-year-old Larry Osborne was sentenced to death on 27 January 1999 in Whitley County. The charges proved were: two counts of intentional murder; first degree burglary; first degree robbery, and first degree arson.

Well done, Larry!

On 14 December 1997, the Whitley County 911 dispatch received a telephone call reporting that the breaking of glass had been heard at a residence and that someone should check out the incident. This message was relayed to the Kentucky State Police and, on arriving at the scene, officers found the place on fire.

The blaze was soon extinguished, and the bodies of Sam and Lillian Davenport were found lying near the front door. A single-barrel shotgun was located about two feet to the right of Sam.

It soon became obvious that the couple had been burgled and a .380-calibre Beretta semi-automatic pistol had been stolen. Osborne was arrested while trying to sell this gun.

This killer advertises on the internet for penpals, saying:

> 'Age 39, Height 5'11', Weight 200, Eyes Hazel, Hair Brown, Seeking friendship. Smile! They're free! I would like to correspond with anyone who needs a penpal to exchange smiles and discourse on anything, from the simple things to the complex, from gardening to geo-political issues. Don't worry, what we don't know about, well, we'll just get a book and learn. I love humor, music, and learning. I have been a lot of places and done a lot of things. How about your big adventure that we call life? I would love to hear all about it. I have worked as a carpenter, promoter, farmer and ran a remolding/building maintenance company. My hobbies are computers, electronics, fishing, camping, and custom woodworking. (All that I can't do here.) I am into martial arts, bodybuilding and fitness. I am currently studying Syda Yoga and Zen Buddhism. I have a fairly wide range of

talents and interests. If you would like to swap ideas, gripes, humor etc. All you need to do is write… Keep the Faith.'

It is notable that nowhere among his richly impressive and varied list of talents and interests does Larry mention killing people and burning houses down. But then he wouldn't, would he?

DAVIS, Henry Alexander (Florida # 358319)
DOB 25.04.1965

This cold-blooded killer who murdered in the furtherance of a robbery is not shy either. Henry Davis advertises on the internet for 'potential friends', modestly describing himself as 'Florida's Finest Chocolate'.

'Hi, my name is Henry,' he says. 'I'm 35 years of age. I have been incarcerated for nearly 13 years on Florida's Death Row. My desire to develop friendship beyond this edifice of political smoke and mirrors is, in part, because I need to dispel the myth that I am void of humanity and, in part, because most of my family and friends are either deceased or have faded away.'

Wrestling clumsily with his vocabulary and losing the battle, Henry continues: 'My basic interests are Law, philosophy, and spirituality. My desire is to meet people who are objectively cogitative on which they can develop a mutually inspiring relationship through some engaging mental intercourse. I welcome women of all races. I weigh 210 lbs. Solid as a rock "smile", healthy, compassionate, sincere, loving, honest and good-looking. For prompt response enclose SASE.'

Were he to reside in the UK, Henry would be guilty of contravening the Trades Descriptions Act, or, at best, of being extremely economical with the truth, for 'Florida's Finest Chocolate' is, after all, proclaiming his virtues from Death Row, where he awaits execution for first degree murder. He is also serving two life sentences, one for the use of a firearm in the execution of his civic duty as a robber and the other for burglary. Two more sentences, each of five years, seem almost too trivial to mention.

His lack of success to date in gaining a pen friend, a source of unhappiness for him, may be due to the prospective applicant's having read the small print on this particular chocolate wrapper or, indeed, having failed to understand what he is talking about!

It goes without saying that thousands of well-meaning, totally honest people feel the need to use the internet to 'adopt' a prisoner on Death Row, or one serving a prison sentence, and good luck to you if you are so inclined. You will find, however, that most proclaim their innocence of the crimes for which they have been convicted; the majority are extremely cunning and, more often than not, will soon be looking for cash handouts.

By all means, surf the net and look up the websites that offer penpal facilities to these criminals – their criminal histories will not feature in most cases – and then, for further advice on specific US inmates, contact the relevant State Department of Corrections. They are all listed on the internet, and most have full details of the offenders, including their crimes, along with photographs.

And, if you bump into the likes of Death Row inmate Charles Ng – who tortured and slaughtered as many as 27 men, women and children – think again, because he wants *you* as a penpal, too.

'I am writing because I am interested in seeking sincere friendship through correspondence and visiting with someone I can build an enduring and meaningful companionship with – someone with whom I can share good times, bad times, life, thoughts, feelings, experiences and passions from this dark hole of humanity.

'Out in the free world I enjoyed such things as reading, learning new subjects, wilderness exploring, martial arts, movies, travelling, cooking, outdoor adventures such as mountain hiking/climbing, scuba diving and serving as an infantryman in the United States Marine Corps.

'Throughout my life I have refrained from unhealthy habits such as smoking, drinking and recreational drug use. During my incarceration I enjoy such things as origami, spirituality, self-study, exercises, writing, reading and drawing. I am a self-taught artist who loves animals and strive to express artistically with an improvisational approach in whatever medium available to me.

'I always feel a special kinship in my struggle for survival with those faced by the endangered animals I depict in my artwork. To me, art is a universal emotional expression of all cultures, and wildlife art a spiritual reference for all things wild and free; and a way for me to immortalize my love and intimacy to those who are dear and special to me. Life is fleeting and my fate is at best uncertain. Therefore, I desire to hear from new friends and reconnect with people who had touched my life and heart in the past, but with whom I have lost touch due to circumstances beyond my control.

'I would be most grateful to be able to share the precious

> time I have left in this world with honest, open-minded and good-hearted people who understand and empathise with injustices, sufferings, my struggle, my visions and yearnings, and who may be able and willing to lend helping hands along the way.'

And here's the punchline:

> 'In order to try and raise money for my day-to-day items and additional art materials I would be prepared to sell a small number of prints of any of my featured drawings. Thank you for your attention and I look forward to hearing from you.'

APPENDIX: HARD FACTS

'I was exposed to pornography for years. It led me to my violent ways.'

SERIAL KILLER TED BUNDY TO DR JAMES DOBSON ON THE NIGHT BEFORE HE WAS EXECUTED IN FLORIDA'S ELECTRIC CHAIR

The internet is a great place to be. Used wisely, with strict controls on which sites are suitable for our children, it can be entertaining, educational and it can bring folk of all races, ethnic groups, religions, pastimes and interests together. And it is now indispensable for global trade; so indispensable, in fact, that, if the internet collapsed tomorrow, the effect, in fiscal terms, would be a thousand times more devastating than the Asian tsunami or Hurricane Katrina.

Of course, the internet will not collapse. Segments of its cell-like structure may do so under the onslaught of a virus, but, in its totality, the web cannot fail. It is here to stay, and millions of people rely on it, almost as much as on the air they breathe and the food they eat.

For good or for bad, the web is the primary means of global communication. It has become a multi-faceted God that we all worship. Conversely, there is the Anti-Christ, and this is what this book is all about.

The journey undertaken throughout this book has been a difficult one, and your authors have arrived at something resembling a conclusion – one that may find favour with many yet receive the disdain of others. But let's not kid ourselves: access to the unfettered freedom and breadth of the web has produced a cyber environment where those with dark, subconscious desires can explore these impulses and even act them out, where the true seed of evil can propagate into flowers of destruction.

Sadly, the cases we have considered above are just the tip of the iceberg, for what follows will shock even the hardened soul.

An article in the *Wall Street Journal* of Monday, 3 May 2004 stated that, after carrying out a ten-year research study of 1,500 sexual addicts, Dr Carnes from Texas estimated that about 8 per cent of men and about 3 per cent of women in the USA are sexually addicted – figures that translate into over 15 million sex addicts.

Citing US Justice Department statistics, it said that in 1998 there were 28,000 X-rated websites, generating a revenue of $925 million in revenue, and only six years later there were ten times as many such websites, generating $10–20 billion. 'Pornography in many forms is invading people's homes and it is available 24 hours a day,' the article concluded.

To even start to comprehend the sums involved, you will need to lie down, take a stiff drink or smoke something illegal about a foot long. Ten to 20 billion dollars! Let's split the difference. Do you have any idea how much $15 billion is? Of course you don't; nobody does. But for a bit of fun let's imagine you are in a vault with that amount of money all about you and you are told that you can keep each dollar bill you can initial. Say, too, for the sake of argument that you could initial one dollar bill each second and that you worked without ever stopping. How long do you think it would take to count $15 billion? Go on, take a guess. Twelve weeks? Five years?

Well, starting in 2005, if you initialled a dollar bill every second you would make $1,000 every 17 minutes. After 12 days' non-stop effort, you would acquire your first $1 million. So it would take you 120 days to accumulate $10 million. After 31.7 years you would become a billionaire, and in 2479 you would have counted your last dollar bill.

Reversing the procedure, if today you started handing back the bills one every second, you wouldn't be destitute until 1530, when Queen Elizabeth I was around and a century before the Mayflower Pilgrims stepped ashore in America.

So the internet sex business is big, but how big?

In fact, this huge, multi-faceted industry is the biggest employer in the world. According to a National Research Council Report published in 2002, the cyber sex industry generates approximately $1 billion annually and this figure is expected to grow to $5–7 billion over the next five years, barring unforeseen change.

The two largest individual buyers of bandwidth in the world are US firms in the adult online industry. Almost from the outset, e-business, especially when it involved sex, was the place to be. To give you a few examples: at the start of 1995, there were just 200 businesses on the web selling 'erotica services' and products, from condoms to pornographic videos. By 1997, it was 14,000. According to Naughty Linx, an online index, in 2004, in excess of eight million sites were selling sex products.

A search for sexual material on Yahoo between August 1995 and August 1996 revealed that in August 1995 the category 'Sex' had 391 listings for phone-sex numbers, adult CD-ROMS, X-rated films, adult computer software, live sex videoconferencing, prostitution tours, escort services and mail-order bride agencies. By August 1996, there were 1,676 listings – a four-fold increase in one year. In 2005, there were 170,000 listings. That is an average of 58 new sites being added each day.

In the UK, there are some 11 million single males. This figure is expected to increase to 16 million by 2010. One in five of them use a dating service, and those figures are expected to double within five years.

These 'punters' are serviced by no fewer than 366,000 British online dating agency listings, and Dating Direct alone boast 1.5 million male and female members on their home page. Worldwide today there are 44 million links to online dating agencies, compared with 13.1 million in March 2003.

Two hundred and fifty million people worldwide use the internet frequently, while an estimated 150,000 new users log on every day.

Figures for the year ending August 2004 show 3.95 million personal advertisements compared with fewer than one million for the previous year; and almost 7.5 million dating services, compared with 2.8 million in 2003.

Fifty-seven million Americans have internet access and 6.5 per cent of *all* male internet users are compulsive cyber-sex addicts hooked on porn sites, X-rated chatrooms or other sexual materials online.

In the UK, at least 550,000 male internet users are hooked on cyber sex.

Cyber sex is the crack cocaine of sexual addiction and it reinforces and normalises sexual disorder. A public health disaster is coming because very few are recognising it as such or taking it seriously.

The MSNBC/Stanford/Duquesne Study, 2000, shows that men prefer visual erotica twice as much as women. Women favour chatrooms twice as much as men. Women have a slightly lower rate of sexually compulsive internet behaviour, and 70 per cent keep their habit a secret.

There are over 120,000 websites – and these are just the advertised sites – dedicated to snuff rape and killings, cannibalism and necrophilia.

Every year many thousands of Western males travel to Eastern Europe, the Far East and Central and South America in search of cheap, most often sordid, sex. One company based in Miami, Florida, offers its clients tours to Costa Rica, the Caribbean and South America and advertises: 'Whatever your personal preference, Latin, blonde, black, mulatto, petite, etc., [the girls] will be friendly, attentive and eager to please you.'

Sexually transmitted diseases caught through sex tourism are reaching epidemic proportions, adding to the 333 million new cases being reported worldwide each year.

Thanks to the criminals who use the internet, the United Nations estimates, between 700,000 and four million women and children are now trafficked around the world for the purposes of forced prostitution, labour and other forms of exploitation every year. Trafficking is, on its own, estimated to be a $7-billion-a-year business. Victims of trafficking are subject to gross human rights violations, including rape, torture, forced abortions, starvation and threats of torture or murder of family members.

Some 2.5 million sites promote 'Boy Sex' and four million advertise 'Extreme Sex'.

Despite a crackdown in recent years, the US Customs Service calculates that there are more than 100,000 websites offering child pornography – which is illegal worldwide. Estimates of the industry's revenue range from about $200 million to more than $1 billion per year. These unlawful sexual images can be purchased as easily as music, DVDs or holidays on the internet. 'Subscribers' typically use credit cards to pay a monthly fee of between $30 and $50 to download photos and videos, or a one-time fee of a few dollars for single images.

The US National Society for the Prevention of Cruelty to Children reported on 8 October 2003, 'More than 20,000 images of child pornography are posted on the internet every week. 140,000 child pornography images were posted to the internet according to researchers who monitored the internet over a six-week period. Twenty children were estimated to have been abused for the first time and more than 1,000 images of each child created and downloaded.'

And America's National Criminal Intelligence Service wrote in August that same year, 'More than half of all illegal sites reported to the Internet Watch Foundation are hosted in the United States. Illegal sites in Russia have more than doubled from 286 to 706 in 2002'

Professor Max Taylor, of Combating Paedophile Information Networks in Europe, stated in March 2003, 'Demand for pornographic images of babies and toddlers on the internet is soaring. More babies and toddlers are appearing on the net and the abuse is getting worse. It is more torturous and sadistic than it was before. The typical age of children is between six and 12, but the profile is getting younger.'

The same report said, 'Approximately 20 new children appear on the porn sites every month – many have been kidnapped or sold into sex.'

Canada faces the same problem. Detective Sergeant Paul Gillespie of Toronto Police Force said, 'In the last couple of years, we've just seen such young children on regular seizures – babies from 2- to 4-year-olds.'

'There was a staggering 345 per cent increase in child pornography sites between February 2001 and July 2001,' according to an August 2001 press release from a web-based internet filtering and monitoring company called N2H2. They also reported 403 child pornography sites, or 67 per month, for the six months April–September 2000. Such sites rose dramatically for the six months February–July 2001 to 1,391, or 231 per month. That's an increase of 345 per cent at the rate of about eight per day.

Perhaps even more disturbing is to learn that there are just under ten million websites dedicated to teen sex, each containing thousands of photographs and hundreds of streaming video clips.

And there are also the collateral financial costs to consider. Billions of dollars and pounds are lost each year to all industries and governments through staff logging on during working hours to surf the internet for sex. Individuals from all walks of life: the judiciary, police, the Church and teachers are hooked on pornography.

Officers from Operation Ore, the UK's largest manhunt for men who visit child porn sites and download illegal material, have already arrested 46 police officers, and the team admit they have not scratched the surface yet. Up to 30 UK police officers a year are being arrested for sexual offences against minors. Most of these offenders had become hooked on internet porn and gone on to play out their fantasies in real life.

Millions are spent by law-enforcement agencies worldwide to detect and bring to justice those who traffic in women and children, and those who view internet child pornography. Astronomical sums are also spent by the judicial systems and the penal systems that have to administer justice and incarcerate offenders, when all of this revenue could be better spent elsewhere.

As we said, this is just the very tip of the iceberg. Unless we wake up, we face a cyber Armageddon.